Japanese Home Style Cooking

Published by Better Home Publishing House

1-15-12 Shibuya, Shibuya-ku
Tokyo 150, Japan

Recipes supplied by The Better Home Association of Japan
Translated by Fumiko Hara
Photography by Hideo Ishizuka
Editor by Mihoko Hoshino

Printed in Japan
First printing, 1986 December 1   Eighteenth printing, 1996 October 20
ISBN4-938508-40-0 C2377

PREFACE

We have the pleasure of presenting to you 61 Japanese home-cooking recipes. A majority of the dishes introduced in this book have been handed down in Japanese homes from generation to generation.

Japan is surrounded by ocean and blessed with four distinct seasons. The daily availability of fresh fish and seasonal vegetables is reflected in the fundamental characteristic of Japanese cooking: food is prepared in a way that will enhance the natural taste and aroma of each ingredient.

Most traditional dishes are made with *dashi* (stock made from dried kelp/bonito fish) and seasoned with unique Japanese fermented items such as soy sauce, *miso* (soybean paste), *sake* (rice wine) and *mirin* (sweet rice wine). Sometimes a small amount of a strong-tasting vegetable is added to give more zest to a dish, as herbs are used in western cooking. Japanese cooking uses oils and fats very sparingly, which is why it is referred to as a low-calorie cuisine.

A standard Japanese meal consists of rice and miso soup plus one main dish with two or more side dishes. Using a variety of cooking methods, Japanese housewives plan their daily menus so as to attain full nutritive values from at least thirty ingredients.

We hope the Japanese dishes introduced here will be tried and enjoyed by all the readers of this book.

The Better Home Association of Japan
(A non-profit foundation)

Contents

Liquid Measures in This Book

1 cup = ½ pint = 240 ml
1 tablespoon = 15 ml
1 teaspoon = 5 ml

Shiso leaves (beefsteak plant)

Kabu (small white turnip)

Japanese-variety pumpkin

Yuzu citron

Japanese-variety eggplant

Ginkgo nuts

Daikon (Japanese radish)

Shungiku (chrysanthemum leaves, edible)

Japanese-variety cucumber

Lotus root

▼10-inch plate
For comparison
of ingredients.

Chinese black mushroom

Japanese

Ingredients

Burdock root

Enokidake (nettle mushroom)

Mitsuba (trefoil)

Long onion

Shimeji mushroom

Wasabi (Japanese horseradish)

Shirataki

Thin deep-fried tofu

Snow peas

(jelly-like noodles made from starch of a vegetable root called devil's tongue)

Kinugoshi-tofu

Grilled *tofu*

Momen-tofu

Sato-imo (taro)

(smooth surface) (rough surface)

Konnyaku (jelly-like cake made from starch of a vegetable root called devil's tongue)

Chinese black mushroom

Chinese black mushroom is used both fresh and dried. Dried Chinese black mushroom makes good soup stock and is often used in soup-based dishes.

Soaking dried Chinese black mushrooms

1 Wash lightly and soak in just enough water to cover till soft. Some weight can be placed on the mushrooms to apply light pressure. A plate can be used to weigh down the mushrooms.
2 Squeeze out water and cut off stems. Keep the water used for soaking to be used for soup stock.

Dried red pepper

Usually dried pods are used in cooking. Be sure to remove seeds as they are very hot. Red pepper is also available in powdered form.

Soaking dried red pepper

1 Soak dried red pepper in water to soften.
2 Cut off tips of both ends and squeeze out seeds under water.

Kampyo (Dried gourd shavings)

Kampyo is made by drying gourd pulp pared into long thin strips. It is boiled to soften before using.

Soaking and boiling kampyo

1 Wet *Kampyo*, sprinkle with salt, and rub well.
2 Rinse in water and boil in plenty of water till soft. Pinch with fingernails; if it tears, it is done.

Sesame seeds

There are black and white sesame seeds. Black sesame has the stronger aroma. Select the color to go with the other ingredients of the dish. Sesame seeds are usually roasted first in order to bring out the aroma and ground in an earthenware mortar. Commercial sesame paste is a handy item for making various sesame dressings.

Roasting sesame seeds

1 Roast sesame seeds in a dry skillet over low heat, stirring constantly to prevent burning.

2 Place the hot roasted sesame seeds in an earthenware mortar and grind with a pestle until the oil seeps out.

2 Place roasted sesame seeds on dry cloth and chop. Half-crushed or chopped sesame seeds are used in dressings and condiments.

Daikon (Japanese radish)

Daikon can be eaten fresh or cooked. Grated *daikon* is called "*daikon-oroshi.*" It is a useful condiment since it helps to neutralize the smell of some ingredients and also aids the digestion. If grated *daikon* is too watery, drain.

Grated *daikon*

Grated *daikon* with red pepper (*Momiji-oroshi*)

Cut *daikon* into 4-inch (10 cm) long pieces; if the daikon is very thick, cut in half. Pare each piece and grate, cut end down.

Pare *daikon* and pierce 2 holes lengthwise with a chopstick. Stuff the two *daikon* holes with dried red pepper (cut in half with seeds removed), and grate together. An easier way to make *momiji-oroshi* is to sprinkle powdered red pepper over grated *daikon*.

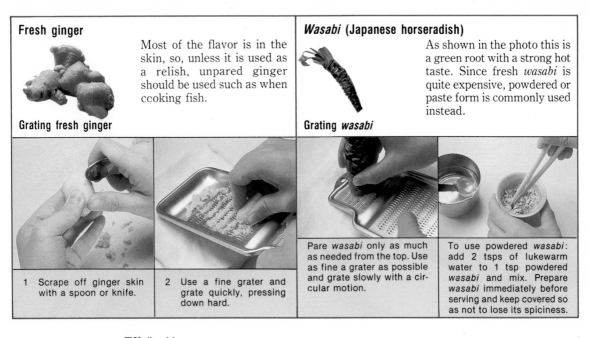

Fresh ginger

Most of the flavor is in the skin, so, unless it is used as a relish, unpared ginger should be used such as when ccoking fish.

Grating fresh ginger

Wasabi (Japanese horseradish)

As shown in the photo this is a green root with a strong hot taste. Since fresh *wasabi* is quite expensive, powdered or paste form is commonly used instead.

Grating *wasabi*

1 Scrape off ginger skin with a spoon or knife.

2 Use a fine grater and grate quickly, pressing down hard.

Pare *wasabi* only as much as needed from the top. Use as fine a grater as possible and grate slowly with a circular motion.

To use powdered *wasabi*: add 2 tsps of lukewarm water to 1 tsp powdered *wasabi* and mix. Prepare *wasabi* immediately before serving and keep covered so as not to lose its spiciness.

Soy sauce

▼Koikuchi shoyu

Soy sauce is made from soybeans and goes very well with almost any ingredient. There are many varieties of soy sauce such as dark colored or light colored, but the most commonly used is *koi-kuchi shoyu* (deep, reddish-brown colored soy sauce).

Rice vinegar

In Japanese cooking rice vinegar is commonly used. Wine vinegar and apple vinegar are not recommended to substitute for rice vinegar as they are too strongly acidic and lack sweetness.

Miso (Soybean paste)

▼Saikyo-miso (sweet white miso

Miso is a seasoning in paste form made from soybeans. It has a salty and unique flavor, and is used primarily in miso soup. It is also used for marinating meats and fish before cooking and as a seasoning in boiled and sauteed dishes.
Saikyo-miso is sweet and less salty not used for *miso* soup unless it is specifically called for. There are many varieties of *miso* ; two or three varieties of *miso* may be blended according to personal taste.

Mirin (Sweet rice wine for cooking)

This is liquid type seasoning made from *mochi gome* (sweet glutinous rice). Its sugar and alcohol contents give a distinctive flavor. *Mirin* is used primarily to add delightful sweetness which sugar alone cannot produce. It is also used to put a finishing gloss on cooked food.

Sake (Rice wine)

As wine is used in French cooking, *sake* is often used in Japanese cooking. For cooking purposes, inexpensive *sake* of any brand will do just as well.

Dried Bonito flakes   *Konbu* (dried kelp)

Dashi (bonito fish stock) is basic to Japanese cooking. In making this stock, the indispensable ingredients are dried bonito flakes and *konbu* (dried kelp). Besides the flakes shown in the photo, bonito in a finely shredded form is also used to be sprinkled on top of a cooked dish.
When using *konbu*, cut into 4-inch (10 cm) lengths. The fine white powder on the surface of the *konbu* contains the essence of the *konbu*'s flavor and should not be washed off.

Sukiyaki

This is a well-known Japanese dish, which is cooked and served at the dinner table.

Ingredients (for 4 persons)

- 1 pound (450g) beef (sirloin, tenderloin or rump) thinly sliced
- 3 long onions
- 10 ounces (300g) *shun-giku* (chrysanthemum leaves, edible/substitute spinach, watercress)
- 8 fresh Chinese black mushrooms
- 1 bundle *shirataki*
- 1 block grilled *tofu*
- 1 chunk beef suet (1 ounce/30g)

Warishita (broth for cooking)

- 1/3 cup (80 ml) soy sauce
- 1/3 cup (80 ml) *mirin*
- 1/3 cup *dashi* (80ml/see page 17)
- 5 tablespoons sugar

- 4 eggs

① Prepare ingredients and arrange on a large plate.
Long onion: cut into diagonal slices, 2-inch (5cm) long.
Fresh Chinese black mushroom: cut off stem and make a criss-cross incision on top (see page 13).
Shirataki : put into boiling water and bring to vigorous boil (picture 1). Drain. Cut into 3–4-inch (8–10cm) lengths (picture 2).
Grilled *tofu* : cut into bite-size pieces.

② Mix all ingredients for *warishita* (cooking broth) and bring to a boil. Pour into a container and set on the dinner table.

③ Heat *sukiyaki* pan on a hot-plate at the dinner table and saute beef suet until half-melted. Add beef, spreading the thin slices. When beef begins to turn color, add a small amount of *warishita* broth, add some of the vegetables and other ingredients. As the ingredients are cooked, the diners serve themselves from the pan; the cooked food is dipped into a lightly whisked egg in an individual bowl. Add more ingredients as the food is eaten. Add *warishita* as it boils off (picture 3). If *warishita* is all gone, *sake* or hot-water can be substituted.

Note: The knack of cooking this dish is to keep the broth 1/4-inch (0.5 cm) deep in the skillet at all times. Divide ingredients into several portions and cook one portion at a time.
If a *sukiyaki* pan is not available, a heavy cast-iron skillet may be used.

1 Preparation of *shirataki*. Put into boiling water and bring to vigorous boil.

2 Bundle and cut into pieces.

3 Add *warishita* as it boils off.

Shabushabu (Beef Slices Cooked in Boiling Broth)

The dish is cooked at the dinner table. Thinly sliced meat held with chopsticks is swished back and forth in the boiling broth for a few seconds; then dipped in the sauce flavored with condiment before eating.

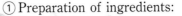

Ingredients (for 4 persons)

1½ pounds (700g) beef
   (sirloin, tenderloin or
   rump)
   sliced paper-thin
4 Chinese cabbage
   leaves
4 ounces (120g) *shun-giku* (chrysanthemum
   leaves, edible)
4 ounces (120g) *seri*
   (watercress)
2 long onions
8 fresh Chinese black
   mushrooms
3½ ounces (100g)
   enokidake (nettle
   mushroom)
2 ounces (60g) *harusame*
6 cups (1.4 l) *dashi* (see
   page 17)

Ponzu-joyu (dipping sauce)
1 tablespoon lemon juice
2 tablespoons rice
   vinegar
5 tablespoons soy sauce
2 -inch (5cm) *konbu*
5 tablespoons *dashi*
2 thin lemon slices

Goma-dare (miso and sesame sauce)
½ cup (50g) white ses-
   ame seeds
3⅓ tablespoons (50g) *miso*
2 tablespoons *mirin*
2 teaspoons soy sauce
2 teaspoons rice vinegar
1 tablespoon grated
   garlic
   red pepper powder
2 teaspoons vegetable
   oil
7 tablespoons *dashi*

Condiments
   grated *daikon* with red
   pepper (see page 6)
   finely chopped scallion

① Preparation of ingredients:
   Beef: Spread out in a large serving dish.
   Chinese cabbage and *shungiku*: boil lightly. Spread 2 cabbage
   leaves on *makisu* (a thin bamboo mat), arrange *shungiku* on top
   at the center and roll up (picture 1). Cut cabbage roll into
   1½-inch (4 cm) lengths.
   Long onion: cut into diagonal slices.
   Chinese black mushrooms: cut off stems and make a crisscross
   incision on the tops (see page 13).
   Enokidake: cut off the bottom part.
   Harusame: soak in lukewarm water and cut into 4-inch (10 cm)
   lengths.

② To make *ponzu-joyu:*
   Mix all ingredients but the sliced lemon and let stand for 10
   minutes. Then remove *konbu* and add sliced lemon.

③ To make *goma-dare*:
   Roast white sesame seeds in dry skillet over low heat until they
   begin to give off aroma. Remove to an earthenware mortar and
   grind until sticky (see page 6). Add white *miso, mirin,* soy sauce,
   vinegar, grated garlic and powdered red pepper and grind further. Then slowly adding vegetable oil and *dashi,* grind until
   smooth.

④ At the dinner table, fill a large pot ¾ full with *dashi* and bring
   to a boil. Add meat and vegetables a little at a time. Add more
   dashi as it boils off. Dip the cooked beef or vegetable into *ponzu-
   joyu* or *goma-dare. Ponzu-joyu* is seasoned with condiments. Skim
   off froth from the surface of broth (picture 2).

Note: In addition to the ingredients listed here, the following are also
        commonly used: chicken breast, chicken liver, pork, white meat
        fish, squid, *toragai* (a shellfish). All ingredients must be sliced very
        thin so they will cook quickly.

1 Spread Chinese cabbage
   leaves on *makisu*, place
   shungiku in the center and
   roll up.

2 Skim off froth.

Yose-nabe (Chicken, Seafood and Vegetables Cooked Together)

This is a hot one-pot dish with a delightful combination of flavors from chicken, seafood and vegetables. It is a Japanese version of bouillabaisse. Cooking is done at the dinner table.

Ingredients (for 4 persons)
- 1 pound (450g) white-meat fish fillets
- ½ pound (230g) chicken, boned
- 8 clams
- 1 squid (body only)
- 8 large shrimps
- 6 Chinese cabbage leaves, large
- 5 ounces (140g) spinach
- 24 *gin-nan* (gingko nuts) boiled
- 7 ounces (200g) *shun-giku* (chrysanthemum leaves, edible)
- 8 fresh Chinese black mushrooms
- 2 ounces (60g) *harusame* (see note)
- 4 cups (960 ml) *dashi* (see page 17)
- 7 tablespoons soy sauce
- 1 tablespoon *mirin*
- 1 tablespoon *sake*

Ponzu-joyu (dipping sauce)
- 1 tablespoon lemon juice
- 2 tablespoons rice vinegar
- 5 tablespoons soy sauce
- 2 -inch (5 cm) piece of *konbu*
- 5 tablespoons *dashi*
- 2 lemon slices

shichimi-togarashi (powdered red pepper mixed with six other spices)

harusame

① Preparation of ingredients:
Fish and chicken: cut into 1½-inch (4 cm) squares.
Clams: soak in slightly salted water for 5–6 hours to remove sand. Rinse well (see page 59).
Squid: peel off skin, cut open and flatten out (see page 65). Cut slashes lengthwise and crosswise. Cut into bite-size pieces and dip through boiling water.
Shrimp: insert toothpick (or skewer) under black vein and remove. Peel off shells, but leave tail (pictures 1 & 2).
Chinese cabbage and spinach: boil lightly. Trim off spinach ends. Spread 2 cabbage leaves on *makisu* (thin bamboo mat), place spinach on top and roll up, and make three cabbage rolls (see page 11). Cut each roll in 1½-inch (4 cm) pieces.
Gin-nan: spear three gingko nuts with a toothpick.
Shungiku: remove stems. Cut leaves into 1½-inch (4 cm) pieces.
Fresh Chinese black mushroom: remove stems. Make a crisscross incision on the tops for a decorative touch (picture 3).
Harusame: soak in lukewarm water and cut into 4-inch (10 cm) lengths.

② *Ponzu-joyu* : mix all ingredients but the sliced lemon and let stand for 10 minutes. Then, remove *konbu* and add sliced lemon.

③ At the dinner table, put *dashi,* soy sauce, *mirin* and *sake* into a large cooking pot and bring to a boil. Put in meat, seafood and vegetables in the order of time required to cook each. When ingredients are cooked, spoon into a small bowl containing *ponzu-joyu* seasoned with *shichimi-togarashi*.

Note: *Harusame* is clear, thin noodles made from a green bean.

1 Remove black vein.

2 Peel shrimp leaving tail section.

3 Make a crisscross incision on the top.

Oden (Meat, Seafood and Vegetables Cooked Together in Soy Sauce Broth)

This dish is similar to a stew in which many kinds of ingredients are cooked together for some time. It is an ideal dish for the cold winter season. The longer it is cooked, the better it tastes.

Ingredients (for 4 persons)
Skewered chicken balls and
grilled tofu
- ¼ pound (120g) chicken,
  ground
- 1 teaspoon fresh ginger
  juice
- 1 tablespoon *sake*
- 1 teaspoon soy sauce
- 1 tablespoon potato or
  corn starch
- 1 block grilled *tofu*

Shinoda-bukuro (stuffed thin
deep-fried *tofu*)
- 2 thin deep-fried *tofu*
- 4 8-inch (20cm) long
  kampyo
- 2 fresh Chinese black
  mushrooms
- 2 ounces (60g) chicken
- 2 ounces (60g) carrot
- ½ bundle *shirataki*

- ½ cup (120 ml) *dashi* (see
  page 17)
- 1 tablespoon soy sauce
- 1 teaspoon *mirin*
- 1 teaspoon *sake*
- salt
- 8 *gin-nan* (gingko nuts)
  canned, boiled

- 1 squid
- 1 pound (450g) *daikon*
  (Japanese radish)
- 1 pound (450g) potato
- 1 block *konnyaku*
- 2-3 5-inch (13cm) long
  konbu

Cooking broth
- 7 cups (1.6 l) *dashi*
- 3 tablespoons soy sauce
- 2 tablespoons *sake*
- 2 tablespoons *mirin*
- 2 teaspoons salt
- Japanese mustard

① Preparation of ingredients:

Skewered chicken balls and grilled *tofu:* mix ground chicken, ginger juice, *sake,* soy sauce, potato starch well till mixture becomes sticky. Make 1-inch (2.5 cm) chicken balls, drop in boiling water and cook till the balls turn whitish; scoop out and drain. Cut grilled *tofu* into blocks same size as chicken balls. Mount chicken balls and *tofu* blocks alternately on skewers.

Shinoda-bukuro (stuffed thin deep-fried *tofu*): soak *kampyo* in water. Cut thin deep-fried *tofu* in half; then open from the cut end to make a sack (see page 35). Pour boiling water over *tofu*. Stuffing: cut mushrooms, chicken, carrots into 1-inch (3 cm) thin strips. Wash *shirataki,* boil in boiling water lightly, and cut into 2-inch (5 cm) pieces (see page 9). Mix *dashi,* soy sauce, *mirin, sake* and a pinch of salt in saucepan and bring to a boil. Add mushrooms, chicken, carrots, *shirataki,* lower heat and simmer until scarcely any broth remains. Stuff *tofu* sacks with the cooked ingredients. Add two *gin-nan* to each sack and tie the end with a strip of *kampyo* (picture 1).

Squid: remove legs and entrails. Cut top part (body) into ¾-inch (2 cm) pieces crosswise. Separate legs into 2–3 leg bunches. Boil squid (body and legs) lightly in slightly salted boiling water.

Daikon: cut into 1-inch (3 cm) pieces crosswise and pare. Round off the cut ends to prevent crumbling while cooking (picture 2). Boil in water used in rinsing rice till slightly softened. If water used in rinsing rice is not available, boil in slightly salted water.

Potato: pare and cut into 2–4 pieces. If small enough, a whole potato can be used. Boil till slightly softened.

Konnyaku: cut into 8 triangles, boil lightly and drain.

Konbu: soak in water to cover till softened. Cut into strips, 1-inch (3 cm) wide. Knot each strip in the center (picture 3). Save the water.

② Add water used for soaking *konbu* to make cooking broth and put in earthenware pot or heavy saucepan. Add seasonings and bring to a boil. Add tied *konbu* and *konnyaku,* lower heat and simmer for 20 minutes. Then add other ingredients and simmer until flavor is well steeped in. Serve with mustard.

Note: In addition to the ingredients listed here, other popular items commonly used are fish paste foods such as fried fish balls, fish dumplings and fish cake.

1 Tie the end of the sack with
  a strip of *kampyo.*

2 Round off the sharp edge of
  the cut end.

3 Tie *konbu* to make a knot.

Clear Soup

The flavor of clear soup depends solely on good stock. You can enjoy many variety of ingredients such as shrimps, clams, seaweeds, bamboo sprouts, radish sprouts, mushrooms, etc.

Ingredients (for 4 persons)
- ½ block *tofu*
- 8 *mitsuba* (trefoil)
- *yuzu* citron
- 2½ cups (600 ml) *dashi* (see page 17)
- ½ teaspoon salt
- 1 teaspoon soy sauce

① Cut *tofu* into a flower shape using a vegetable cutter.
② Rub *mitsuba* stalks between the fingers to soften, and knot in the center.
③ Pare off thin peel from *yuzu* citron and cut into 4 thin pieces.
④ Make *dashi* stock. Bring *dashi* to a boil; season with salt and soy sauce.
⑤ Place *tofu* and *mitsuba* gently in a soup bowl. Pour in hot *dashi* carefully and float a piece of *yuzu* citron peel.

How To Make Dashi (Bonito Fish Stock)

Dashi is an essential element in many Japanese dishes. It provides a savory flavor which cannot be attained by using seasonings only and it is much easier to make than meat stock.

Here, we would like to show you how to make 2 kinds of *dashi*: one is made from *konbu* and dried bonito flakes; the other is made from bonito flakes only. The former is richer in flavor, so it is recommended for use in a dish where the soup itself is the main ingredient to be enjoyed.

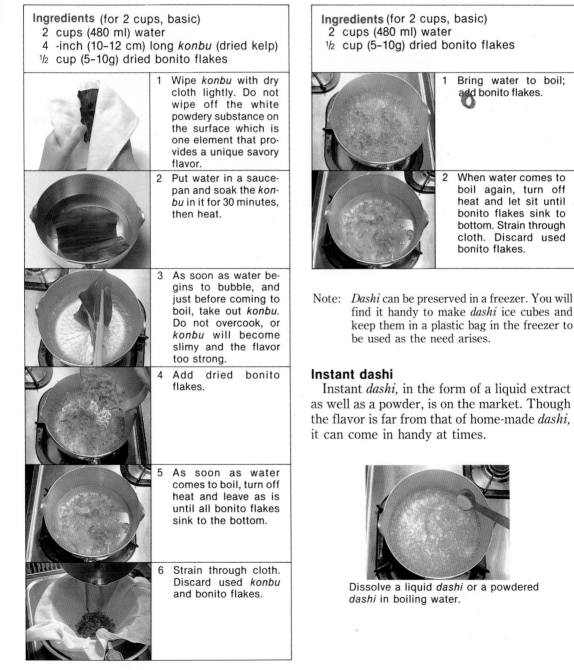

Dashi made from konbu and dried bonito flakes

Ingredients (for 2 cups, basic)
- 2 cups (480 ml) water
- 4 -inch (10-12 cm) long *konbu* (dried kelp)
- ½ cup (5-10g) dried bonito flakes

1. Wipe *konbu* with dry cloth lightly. Do not wipe off the white powdery substance on the surface which is one element that provides a unique savory flavor.

2. Put water in a saucepan and soak the *konbu* in it for 30 minutes, then heat.

3. As soon as water begins to bubble, and just before coming to boil, take out *konbu*. Do not overcook, or *konbu* will become slimy and the flavor too strong.

4. Add dried bonito flakes.

5. As soon as water comes to boil, turn off heat and leave as is until all bonito flakes sink to the bottom.

6. Strain through cloth. Discard used *konbu* and bonito flakes.

Dashi made from dried bonito flakes

Ingredients (for 2 cups, basic)
- 2 cups (480 ml) water
- ½ cup (5-10g) dried bonito flakes

1. Bring water to boil; add bonito flakes.

2. When water comes to boil again, turn off heat and let sit until bonito flakes sink to bottom. Strain through cloth. Discard used bonito flakes.

Note: *Dashi* can be preserved in a freezer. You will find it handy to make *dashi* ice cubes and keep them in a plastic bag in the freezer to be used as the need arises.

Instant dashi

Instant *dashi,* in the form of a liquid extract as well as a powder, is on the market. Though the flavor is far from that of home-made *dashi,* it can come in handy at times.

Dissolve a liquid *dashi* or a powdered *dashi* in boiling water.

Miso Soup

Miso soup almost invariably accompanies a Japanese style meal. *Miso* paste is made from soybeans which are full of high-quality vegetable protein; therefore, *miso* soup is an excellent health food.

Ingredients (for 4 persons)
2½ cups (600ml) *dashi* (see page 17)
½ block *tofu*
    (6 ounces/170g)
3-4 tablespoons *miso*
1 sheet thin deep-fried *tofu*
1 scallion, chopped

① Make *dashi* (see page 17).

② Cut *tofu* into half-inch cubes. Pour boiling water over thin deep-fried *tofu* to remove excess oil; cut in half lengthwise and cut each piece into ½-inch (1 cm) strips.

③ Dissolve *miso* paste by stirring in a small amount of *dashi* broth bit by bit.

④ Heat broth, add thin deep-fried *tofu* and boil lightly. Blend in dissolved *miso* paste and add *tofu* (see note/picture 1).

⑤ Bring to boil and immediately turn off heat. Ladle *miso* soup into individual serving bowls and garnish with chopped scallions.

Note: Ingredients requiring longer cooking time should be cooked in the broth before adding *miso* paste. Add ingredients which cook quickly, such as *tofu* and seaweed, with the *miso*, bring to boil and immediately turn off heat.

Other popular ingredients for *miso* soup include thinly cut *daikon*, *kabu* (turnips), potatoes, snow peas, onions and eggplant.

Just as with toasted croutons in a cream soup the taste of *miso* soup is enhanced by sprinkling condiments to add a bit of flavor and color. Such condiments as *shichimi-togarashi* (powdered red pepper mixed with six other spices), *shiso* leaves, fresh ginger, sesame seeds, *nori*, sprouts, *yuzu* citron peel are recommended.

1 Blend in dissolved *miso* paste.

How To Cook Rice

Rice is the principal staple food in Japan and is cooked every day in most homes. In recent years automatic electric rice cookers have come into wide use. Yet, people who insist on the best tasting rice still prefer using a heavy iron cooking pot.

The kind of rice eaten in Japan is the short-grained variety, which can be cooked to a fluffy texture with just the right amount of moisture.

Ingredients (for 4 persons)
2½ cups (480g) short-grain rice
3 cups (720 ml) water

1   Mix rice lightly in plenty of water and immediately drain. Then put rice back into the pot.

2   Stir as you press rice hard with the palm of your hand, add water and rinse out white water. Repeat 3-4 times until water becomes almost clear, then drain.

3   Add 3 cups (720 ml) of water and leave for 30-60 minutes.

4   Place pot on stove and cook over medium to low heat for 10 minutes, gradually bringing to vigorous boil; then reduce heat to keep water from bubbling over.
Keep boiling for 4-5 minutes; then reduce heat to very low and simmer for a further 15 minutes. Turn heat to high for the last 5 seconds to evaporate excess water, and turn off heat. Let stand and steam for 10 minutes with lid tightly closed.

5   Remove lid quickly, so as not to let drops of moisture fall from lid onto rice, and let steam escape. Wet a wooden spatula and mix rice lightly with folding motion from the bottom up to make it fluffy. Dish out into individual bowls. Cover any rice remaining in pot with cloth and replace lid.
If core of cooked rice remains hard, it needs more moisture. Sprinkle with *sake* (1 tablespoon *sake* per 2½ cups of rice) and simmer on low heat 7-8 minutes.

Note: After steaming rice, transfer rice into *ohitsu* (wooden rice tub). Insert dry cloth under lid and let stand for 5-10 minutes. This way you can enjoy the fullest taste of cooked rice.
Ohitsu is made of soft, plain wood and is specifically designed for keeping cooked rice. The soft wood material absorbs excess moisture from rice and keeps it in the best possible condition.

Ten-don (Rice Topped with Tempura)

Gyu-don (Rice Topped with Beef)

This dish is served by topping fried shrimp or cooked beef over steaming hot rice in a bowl. Leftover *tempura* or *sukiyaki* can be used to easily make similar dishes.

Ten-don (Rice Topped with Tempura

Ingredients (for 4 persons)
   4 bowls of cooked rice
      (see page 19)
   8 shrimps (2½–3
      ounces/80g each)
   ½ cup egg and cold
      water mixture
      (½ egg)
   ½ cup (60g) flour
   vegetable oil for deep-
      frying
Ten-tsuyu (sauce)
   ⅔ cup (160 ml) *dashi* (see
      page 17)
1½ tablespoons sugar
   3 tablespoons soy sauce
   3 tablespoons *mirin*

① Cook rice.
② Remove black vein of shrimp inserting toothpick between shell segments (see page 13). Peel shrimp, leaving tail and the first section of shell attached to tail. Make 3–4 short cuts across the belly to prevent curling while being fried. Trim tip of tail and squeeze out water to prevent popping during frying (picture 1).
③ To make *ten-tsuyu* : mix *dashi*, sugar, soy sauce and *mirin* in saucepan and bring to a boil; then simmer 2–3 minutes.
④ Mix egg and cold water in mixing bowl. Add flour and mix lightly. The knack is to mix lightly so as not to get flour sticky (picture 2).
⑤ Heat vegetable oil to 340°F (170°C). Dip shrimp in batter and fry (see page 94).
⑥ Place cooked rice in a serving bowl. Dip the fried shrimp in the *ten-tsuyu* and place on top of rice. Ladle 2 tablespoons of *ten-tsuyu* over the topping.

Gyu-don (Rice Topped with Beef)

Ingredients (for 4 persons)
   4 bowls of cooked rice
      (see page 19)
   ½ pound (230g) beef,
      thinly sliced
   2 long onions
   1 bundle *shirataki*
   ½ cup (60g) sugar
   3 tablespoons *mirin*
   ½ cup (120 ml) soy sauce

① Cook rice.
② Cut thinly sliced beef into 1½-inch (4 cm) pieces.
   Cut long onion diagonally into 1½-inch pieces.
   Put *shirataki* into boiling water and bring to a boil; then drain.
   Cut into 2-inch (5 cm) lengths.
③ Mix sugar, *mirin* and soy sauce in saucepan and bring to a boil. Add beef; remove as soon as color changes. Add long onion, and *shirataki* and simmer for 3–4 minutes, then put back the beef and cook lightly.
④ Place cooked rice in a serving bowl and place ingredients on top. Ladle 2 tablespoons of sauce over the topping.

1   Squeeze out water from the tip of tail.

2   Add flour to the egg/water mixture. The batter can be lumpy.

Rice Cooked with Chicken and Vegetables

This dish, rice cooked with chicken and vegetables, becomes a light meal in itself if served with a bowl of clear soup and a dish of pickles on the side. Ingredients appropriate to each season are used—fresh green peas for spring, various mushrooms and nuts for autumn.

Ingredients (for 4 persons)

2½ cups (480g) short-grain rice

2½ cups (600ml) *dashi,* containing the water used for soaking mushrooms (see page 17)

6 tablespoons *sake*

2 tablespoons soy sauce

⅔ teaspoon salt

2 ounces (60g) burdock root

4 dried Chinese black mushrooms

½ block (about 4 ounces/120g) *konnyaku*

2 ounces (60g) carrot

4 ounces (120g) chicken, boned and skinned

1 sheet thin deep-fried *tofu*

5 tablespoons green peas (canned or frozen)

① Wash rice and rinse well. Soak in water for 30 minutes and drain.

② To prepare ingredients:

Burdock: scrape off the thin, brown skin with back of knife and shave into thin pieces. Soak in water immediately to prevent discoloration (picture 1).

Dried black Chinese mushrooms: wash lightly and soak in just enough water to cover (see page 6). Squeeze out water and cut into thin strips. Keep the water used for soaking.

Konnyaku: cut in half crosswise; then cut sideways into 3 slices. Cut slices into strips. Boil lightly (picture 2) and drain.

Carrots: cut into thin 1-inch (2.5 cm) strips.

Chicken: cut into ½-inch (1 cm) pieces.

Thin deep-fried *tofu*: pour boiling water over fried *tofu* to remove excess oil. Cut in half lengthwise; then cut each piece into thin strips crosswise.

③ Put rice in heavy saucepan. Add all ingredients, 2½ cups *dashi* (containing the water used for soaking mushrooms), *sake,* soy sauce, salt and mix. Cook the rice mixture the same way as plain rice is cooked (see page 19).

④ Pour boiling water over green peas. When rice mixture is cooked turn off heat, place green peas on top, re-cover tightly and steam for 10–15 minutes to fluff up the rice. Before serving, mix rice and ingredients with a folding motion.

1 Soak burdock shavings immediately in water.

2 Boil *konnyaku* lightly.

Sekihan (Rice Cooked with Azuki Beans)

Azuki beans give a reddish color to the rice, which is why this dish is often prepared for celebrations in Japan. When we say, "Let's have *sekihan*," we mean we intend to celebrate something.

It is good to eat immediately after cooking but is also quite tasty even cold.

Ingredients (for 4 persons)
2½ cups (17 ounces/480g)
    glutinous rice
⅕ cup (40g) *azuki* beans
1 tablespoon black
    sesame seeds
⅔ teaspoon salt

① Wash glutinous rice, stirring gently by hand and rinse 3–4 times (see page 19). Soak in water for 2 hours; then drain.

② Put *azuki* beans in water to cover. Bring to a boil and drain. Then add 3 cups (720 ml) water and simmer for 30 minutes on low heat. Do not overcook. Beans should retain a slight hardness. (Pinch bean between fingers to test) Drain, reserving the reddish water (picture 1). Adding water if necessary, bring the reddish water used for boiling beans to measure 1⅗ cups (380 ml).

③ Put rice, *azuki* beans and 1⅗ cups of water used for boiling beans in heavy saucepan and mix (picture 2). Cover with a tight-fitting lid and bring to vigorous boil; then reduce heat to keep water from bubbling out and simmer 10 minutes. Mix quickly then simmer for a further 10 minutes. Turn heat to high for 5 seconds to evaporate excess water and turn off heat. Then remove lid to let steam out, mix rice gently with folding motion from the bottom up.

④ Sprinkle with roasted sesame seeds and salt.
To make roasted sesame seeds and salt:
Roast black sesame seeds in a dry skillet over low heat, stirring constantly to prevent burning. When seeds begin to give off aroma, add salt and roast together for 5 seconds (picture 3). Remove to a dish.

Note: Roasted sesame seeds and salt help enhance the taste of cooked rice. It can be sprinkled over rice balls or plain rice in a bowl or in a lunch box. Keep in a tightly capped bottle to prevent its getting damp.

1 Drain and keep the water used for boiling.

2 Put rice, *azuki* beans and 1⅗ cups of water used for boiling *azuki* beans.

3 Add salt and roast for 5 seconds.

Ocha-zuke (Clear Rice Soup)

Tai-chazuke

Salmon-chazuke

Beef-chazuke

This dish is made by sprinkling ingredients on top of steaming hot rice in a bowl and pouring piping hot clear soup or Japanese tea over everything. The plain and simple taste of *ocha-zuke* is especially enjoyable after drinking a good bit of *sake* or eating a rich feast.

Ingredients (for 4 persons)
For each chazuke
4 bowls hot cooked rice
(¾ full)

Clear soup
6 cups *dashi* (see page 17)
1 teaspoon salt
1½ teaspoons soy sauce

① To make clear soup:
Make *dashi* with *konbu* (dried kelp) and bonito flakes (see page 17). Flavor with salt and soy sauce.
② Cooked rice must be steaming hot for this dish. If rice is cold, warm in a steamer or in a micro-wave oven.

Note: *Ocha-zuke* with clear soup is usually accompanied with more sophisticated ingredients. With simple ingredients such as pickles or *tsukudani* (various foods boiled down in soy sauce), a plain Japanese tea is used, making a simple but tasty dish.

Tai-chazuke (for 4 persons)
1 fillet (5 ounces/140g) *tai* (sea bream) for *sashimi*
1 tablespoon white sesame seeds
mitsuba (trefoil)
wasabi, grated or paste

① To prepare ingredients:
Tai (sea bream): cut into very-thin slices (picture 1).
Sesame seeds: roast in dry skillet. Place on dry cloth and crush coarsely with knife (see page 6).
Mitsuba : cut into 1-inch (2.5 cm) lengths.
② Put rice in individual serving bowls, place *tai, mitsuba,* sesame and *wasabi* on top and pour in hot clear soup.

Note: Leftovers from tuna *sashimi* (see page 50) will make an equally delightful dish. The tuna should be steeped in soy sauce for a while before placing on the rice.

Salmon-chazuke (for 4 persons)
2 fillets (7 ounces/200g) salmon
1 teaspoon salt
½ sheet toasted *nori* (dried laver)
1 tablespoon white sesame seeds
mitsuba
fresh ginger juice (see page 49)

① To prepare ingredients:
Salmon: sprinkle with 1 teaspoon salt and refrigerate for 12 hours. Then grill and break into small pieces while warm (picture 2).
Nori (dried laver): cut into thin pieces with scissors or crumple up into pieces in a plastic bag (picture 3).
Sesame seeds: roast and crush (see page 6).
Mitsuba : cut into 1-inch (2.5 cm) lengths.
② Put rice in individual serving bowls, place salmon, sesame, *mitsuba* and *nori* on top, pour in hot clear soup and sprinkle with ginger juice.

Note: For salmon-*chazuke,* Japanese tea may be used in place of clear soup.

Beef-chazuke (for 4 persons)
5 ounces (140g) lightly grilled rare (see page 36), or roast beef
1 tablespoon white sesame seeds
chopped scallions
wasabi, grated or paste

① To prepare ingredients:
Beef: cut into thin strips.
Sesame seeds: roast and crush (see page 6).
Scallions: chop crosswise.
② Put rice in individual serving bowls, place beef, scallions, sesame seeds and *wasabi* on top and pour in hot clear soup.

1 Cut *tai* into thin slices.

2 Break grilled salmon into small pieces.

3 Cut *nori,* or crumple up.

Nigiri-zushi (Hand-formed Sushi)

This is a well-known Japanese dish, consisting of vinegared rice formed by hand into small rectangular blocks and topped with various kinds of raw fish, etc.

Ingredients (for 4 persons, 45–50 pieces)

Sushi rice

- 2½ cups (480g) short-grain rice
- 2½ cups (600ml) water
- 2½ -inch (6cm) long *konbu*

Vinegar dressing

- 1 tablespoon sugar
- 4⅔ tablespoons (70ml) rice vinegar
- 1½ teaspoons salt

Tane (ingredients for top pieces)

- 3 ounces (90g) tuna, 4 slices
- 1½ ounces (50g) *tai* (sea bream), 4 slices
- 1½ ounces (50g) squid, sliced 4 pieces
- 4 ark shells
- 4 shrimps (vinegar dressing; 4 tablespoons rice vinegar, 1⅓ tablespoons sugar ½ teaspoon salt)
- 4 tablespoons *uni* (sea urchin roe)
- 4 tablespoons salmon roe
- 4 pieces *anago* (a variety of eel) 5-inch/13cm long, grilled (3 tablespoons *dashi*, ⅔ tablespoon sugar, 1⅓ tablespoons soy sauce, 1⅓ tablespoons *mirin*)

① Make *sushi* rice flavored with vinegar (see page 31).

② To prepare ingredients for topping:
Shrimp: remove black vein (see page 13), pass a bamboo skewer through to keep from curling (picture 1), put in a saucepan containing enough water to cover mixed with 1 tablespoon *sake* and a pinch of salt, and boil. Remove from saucepan, rotate the skewer and cool. Remove skewer, peel but leave tail. Open the belly side lengthwise to flatten out. Steep in vinegar dressing.
Grilled *anago*: cook in *dashi* mixed with sugar, soy sauce and *mirin* over medium heat until *dashi* mixture thickens and volume is reduced. Cut *anago* into 1¼-inch (3 cm) pieces.
Egg: cook as shown on page 86. Cut into ½-inch (1 cm) pieces.
Nori: cut some sheets into 1×6-inch (2.5×15 cm) pieces for wrapping *uni* and salmon roe, and others into ½×6-inch (1×15 cm) pieces for wrapping egg.

③ Wet hands with a mixture of equal parts of vinegar and water. Scoop up a small amount of rice (one or two bite-size / picture 2). Transfer the rice into the space formed by bending the fingers of the left hand half-way. Form the rice into a rectangular shape with help of the right index finger and middle finger by pressing lightly (picture 3). Garnish inside a piece of raw fish with a little *wasabi* (picture 4), place the formed rice on top and press fish and rice together lightly (picture 5).

④ *Uni*: wrap a piece of *nori* around the side of formed rice and place *wasabi* and *uni* on top (picture 6).
Salmon roe: wrap a piece of *nori* around the side of formed rice, place salmon roe.

Egg: place egg on top of formed rice and wrap a strip of *nori* at the middle.

Anago: place *anago* on top of formed rice and brush some of the sauce used for cooking *anago* over the top.

1 Pass through a bamboo skewer.

2 Scoop up rice and press lightly.

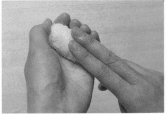

3 Press lightly with two fingers.

4 Garnish tane with *wasabi*.

5 Place the formed rice on *tane*, pressing lightly.

6 Wrap *nori* around the side of rice and place *uni*.

4 slices fried egg fla-
   vored with *dashi* (see
   page 86)
1¼ sheets toasted *nori*
   (dried laver)
wasabi, grated or paste
sweet marinated ginger
soy sauce

Note: Be sure to choose very fresh raw fish. The size of the topping is about 1¼-inch (3 cm) wide, 2½-inch (6.5 cm) long and ¼-inch (0.5 cm) thick.

Do not use *wasabi* for egg or *anago*.

Nigiri-zushi is lightly dipped in the soy sauce.

Temaki-zushi (Hand-wrapped Sushi)

Ingredients (for 4 persons, about 40 pieces)
Sushi rice
2½ cups (480g) short-grain
   rice
2½ cups (600 ml) water
2½ -inch (6 cm) long
   konbu
Vinegar dressing
1 tablespoon sugar
4⅔ tablespoons (70ml) rice
   vinegar
1½ teaspoons salt
10 sheets toasted *nori*
   (dried laver), (stan-
   dard size 7 × 8
   inches/18 × 20cm)
Tane (ingredients for center)
¾ pound (340g) very fresh
   tuna
5 ounces (140g) very
   fresh squid
1 ounce (30g) salmon roe
2 ounces (60g) salted
   cod roe
1 pack (1⅓ ounces/40g)
   natto (fermented
   soybeans)
Japanese mustard
1 Japanese-variety
   cucumber
   (4 ounces/120g)
6 -inch long pickled
   daikon (Japanese
   radish)
1 tablespoon roasted
   white sesame seeds
10 *shiso* leaves (beefsteak
   plant)
½ pack radish sprouts
1 *ume-boshi* (pickled
   Japanese apricot)
wasabi, grated or paste
soy sauce

Place *sushi* rice and ingredients on *nori*.

① Cook *sushi* rice (see page 31). Cut each sheet of *nori* in quaters.

② To prepare ingredients:
Tuna: cut into ½ × ½ × 2½-inch (1 × 1 × 6.5 cm) blocks.
Squid: cut into ½ × 2½-inch (1 × 6.5 cm) pieces.
Cod roe: peel off thin skin.
Natto : chop and mix with mustard.
Cucumber: cut diagonally into thin slices. Cut slices into thin strips and mix with ½ tablespoon sesame seeds.
Pickled *daikon* : cut into thin strips and mix with ½ tablespoon sesame seeds.
Radish sprouts: cut off roots.
Ume-boshi : remove seed and chop.

③ Place *sushi* rice and ingredients on separate serving dishes and set at the table. Each person takes up a sheet of *nori,* places rice (a bite size) and his/her choice of ingredient on the *nori* and wraps it up (see inset). This is lightly dipped into a small dish containing soy sauce just before eating.

Note: *Nori* absorbs moisture very easily and thus loses its crispness, so keep it in its air-tight can until immediately before eating.

Other suggested ingredients are cheese, ham, various sausages, anchovy and avocado.

How To Make Sushi Rice (Vinegar Flavored Rice)

Vinegar flavored rice is used in a variety of *sushi* dishes such as *Nigiri-zushi, Temaki-zushi,* etc. *Sushi* rice is made by sprinkling vinegar dressing over cooked rice and mixing together quickly. Ingredients for vinegar dressing vary slightly depending on the kind of *sushi* dish.

1 The method of cooking rice for *sushi* dishes is the same as that of cooking plain, regular rice (see page 19). The only difference is that *konbu* is added and boiled together with the rice. *Konbu* should be removed as soon as water reaches a vigorous boil. *(Konbu must be taken out very quickly so that the lid may be replaced immediately.)*

2 Mix ingredients to make vinegar dressing.

Note: As with *ohitsu* (see page 19), *sushi-oke* absorbs excess moisture from *sushi* rice. *Sushi-oke* is specifically designed for mixing rice and vinegar dressing in it. If *sushi-oke* is not available, a flat, large pan or tray will do. An electric hair dryer is a convenient device for cooling the rice.

3 After turning off heat, allow rice to steam for an additional 10 minutes. Then empty into *sushi-oke* (large wooden tub). Sprinkle vinegar dressing over rice.

4 Cooling rice with a fan, mix with wet wooden spatula in a cutting manner. Quick cooling gives a glossy texture to the rice.

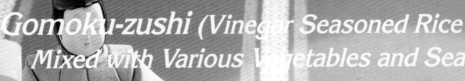

Gomoku-zushi (Vinegar Seasoned Rice Mixed with Various Vegetables and Seafood)

A colorful and eye-pleasing dish, Gomoku-zushi is a party favorite.

Ingredients (for 4 persons)

2½ cups (480g) short-grain
 rice
2½ cups (600ml) water
2½ -inch (6cm) long *konbu*
Vinegar dressing
4⅔ tablespoons rice
 vinegar
 2 tablespoons sugar
1½ teaspoons salt
Ingredients for mixing
 7 dried Chinese black
 mushrooms,
 softened
⅓ ounce (10g) *kampyo*,
 rubbed and boiled
⅔ cup (160 ml) *dashi* (see
 page 17), including
 water used for soak-
 ing mushrooms
1½ tablespoons sugar
½ tablespoon *mirin*
 1 tablespoon (slightly
 less) soy sauce

 3 ounces (90g) lotus root
 2 tablespoons *dashi*
 2 tablespoons sugar
 3 tablespoons rice vinegar
 1 tablespoon *sake*
 salt

 2 ounces (60g) carrot
¼ cup (60 ml) *dashi*
 1 teaspoon *mirin*

 3 eggs
 1 teaspoon potato or
 corn starch
 1 teaspoon sugar
 1 tablespoon *mirin*

1½ ounces (50g) snow
 peas
 2 tablespoons white ses-
 ame seeds
3½ ounces (100g) crab
 meat (canned)
 red pickled ginger
 1 sheet toasted *nori*
 (dried laver)

① Make sushi rice flavored with vinegar (see page 31).

② To prepare ingredients: (picture 2)
 Chinese black mushrooms and *kampyo* (see page 6): cut off stems of mushrooms and cut caps into thin strips.
 In a saucepan make ⅔ cup (160 ml) *dashi,* add mushrooms and *kampyo* and boil with a lid placed right on the ingredients (see page 71) for 3–4 minutes. Add sugar and *mirin* and boil for another 5 minutes, then add soy sauce. When *kampyo* is well flavored, remove from saucepan. Continue to cook mushrooms until broth is all gone. Cut *kampyo* into ½-inch (1 cm) long thin strips.
 Lotus root : Pare and cut into 4 pieces lengthwise. Cut each piece into thin slices crosswise and soak in water. Cook in *dashi* broth with sugar, vinegar, *sake* and a pinch of salt until all liquid is gone.
 Carrots: cut into 1-inch (2.5 cm) long thin strips. Cook in *dashi* broth with *mirin* and a pinch of salt until all liquid is gone.
 Eggs: To whisked egg add potato or corn starch mixed with an equal volume of water, sugar, *mirin* and a pinch of salt. Heat 1 tablespoon of vegetable oil, spreading it out in skillet. Remove excess oil. Turn heat to low and spoon in a small amount of egg mixture, spreading it out to cover the surface of skillet thinly, and fry. When the under side is done, turn over and fry lightly (picture 1). Repeat and make 4–5 thin sheets of fried egg. Cut sheets into thin strips.
 Snow peas: string and boil lightly till tender-crisp. Cut diagonally into thin strips.
 White sesame: roast and crush coarsely with knife (see page 6).
 Crab: remove from can and flake.
 Red pickled ginger and toasted *nori* : cut into thin strips.

③ Add all prepared ingredients except red pickled ginger, *nori,* one-half of the egg strips and the snow peas to *sushi* rice and mix quickly in a chopping motion with wooden spatula (picture 3).

④ Place the *sushi* rice mixture in a large serving dish and on top nicely arrange the remaining egg, snow peas, red pickled ginger and *nori.*

2 All ingredients are prepared.

3 Add ingredients to vinegar-seasoned rice and mix.

1 Carefully turn over and fry lightly.

Inari-zushi (Vinegar Flavored Rice Wrapped In Fried Tofu)

Maki-zushi (Rolled Sushi)

Thin deep-fried *tofu* cooked and flavored is made into a sack and stuffed with *sushi* rice. *Maki-zushi* is made by wrapping *nori* around a *sushi* rice roll with ingredients in the center. Both kinds of *sushi* are often prepared for picnic lunches.

Inari-zushi

Ingredients (for 4 persons)
Sushi rice
1²/₃ cups (320g) short-grain
   rice
1²/₃ cups (400ml) water
1½ -inch (4cm) long *konbu*
Vinegar dressing
   3 tablespoons rice
      vinegar
   4 teaspoons sugar
   1 teaspoon salt
  10 sheets thin deep-fried
      tofu
1¼ cups (300ml) *dashi*
   3 tablespoons sugar
   2 tablespoons soy sauce
   1 tablespoon *mirin*

Maki-zushi

Ingredients (for 4 persons)
Sushi rice (same as page 33)
Vinegar dressing (same as
   page 33)
   6 dried Chinese black
      mushrooms, softened
      (see page 6)
  ½ ounce (15g) *kampyo,*
      boiled (see page 6)
   1 cup (240 ml) *dashi* (see
      page 17)
2½ tablespoons sugar
  ⅓ teaspoon salt
   2 teaspoons soy sauce
   5 ounces (140g) spinach,
      boiled
  ½ teaspoon soy sauce
   3 eggs
   1 tablespoon sugar
soy sauce
   5 sheets toasted *nori*
      (dried laver)

① Make *sushi* rice flavored with vinegar (see page 31).
② Tap fried *tofu* with side of knife. Cut in half and carefully open the cut end to make a sack (picture 1). Pour boiling water over the *tofu* to remove excess oil.
③ Mix *dashi,* sugar, soy sauce and *mirin* in saucepan and bring to a boil. Put *tofu* sacks in the boiling mixture and place a lid right on the *tofu* (see page 71). Simmer until all liquid is absorbed.
④ Stuff *sushi* rice into *tofu* sacks ¾ full. Fold the sack end to close and place in a serving dish with the folded side underneath.

① Make *sushi* rice flavored with vinegar.
② To prepare ingredients for center of rolls:
Chinese black mushrooms and *kampyo*: cut mushrooms into thin strips. Cook *kampyo* and mushrooms in *dashi* broth flavored with sugar, salt and soy sauce.
Spinach: sprinkle with soy sauce.
Egg: whisk egg and mix with sugar and a dash of soy sauce. Heat skillet, spread oil, pour in egg mixture and cook, making a ½-inch (1cm) thick piece. Cut into ½-inch wide strips.
③ Place *nori* on *makisu* (thin bamboo mat) with the shiny side down. Spread out ⅕ *sushi* rice on *nori* evenly, press lightly with fingers moistened in vinegar-water. Leave ½-inch space at near side and 1-inch (2.5 cm) space at far end (picture 2).
④ On top of *sushi* rice place ⅕ the volume of each of all ingredients (picture 3).
⑤ Lift the near end of *makisu,* fold over rice and ingredients and press. Pulling the *makisu* up and away from you to keep the *nori* from wrinkling, continue folding and make into a roll (pictures 4 & 5).
Adjust the shape of rolled rice and remove the roll from *makisu.* Push back protruding rice from both ends of roll into the roll.
⑥ Moving knife lightly, cut *sushi* roll, taking care not to squash it. After each cutting, knife should be wiped with wet cloth.

1 Open the cut end to make a sack.

2 Spread out *sushi* rice. Leave some empty space at both ends.

3 Arrange ingredients.

4 Lifting the nearest end of *makisu,* fold over rice and ingredients and press.

5 Pulling the *makisu* end up, form rice into roll.

Beef Tataki (Lightly Grilled Rare Beef with Condiments)

It is a perfect dish for parties. The best quality meat being used, this dish is a big treat in Japan, for beef is quite expensive.

Ingredients (for 4 persons)

¾ pound (340g) beef (tenderloin)

Condiments

4 tablespoons finely chopped scallions

1 lemon

2 teaspoons grated garlic

2 teaspoons grated fresh ginger (see page 6)

7 ounces (200g) *daikon* (Japanese radish)

1 Japanese-variety cucumber (4 ounces/120g)

shiso leaves (beefsteak plant)

soy sauce

① Heat grid well. Place beef on grid and grill on all sides (picture 1). When the surface turns light brown, dip in ice water for a few seconds. Dry with a cloth, wrap in saranwrap and place in the refrigerator.

② Prepare condiments. Cut lemon into 8 wedges.

Pare *daikon* into paper thin sheets, cutting with bottom part of knife while rotating the *daikon*. Roll *daikon* sheet and slice thinly crosswise, thus making very thin and long strips (pictures 2 & 3). (If this cutting method is too difficult, cut *daikon* into very thin 2-inch/5 cm long strips.) Do the same with cucumber.

③ Cut beef into thin slices. Place *daikon* strips, cucumber and beef slices in a serving dish. Put other condiments on the side. Place scallions on beef. Pour soy sauce into small individual serving dishes and add condiments to taste. The beef is dipped lightly in the soy sauce.

1 Grill beef on all sides.

2 Pare *daikon* into paper thin sheets.

3 Roll *daikon* sheet and slice thinly crosswise.

Niku-jaga (Flavored Meat and Potatoes)

Beef Flavored with Soy Sauce and Ginger

Niku-jaga is one of the most popular everyday dishes in Japanese homes. Fatty pork or beef is recommended for this dish.

Beef flavored with soy sauce and ginger goes very well with rice. Refrigerated, this dish keeps for 5 days and comes in handy for to dress up a meal when the menu seems less than adequate.

Niku-jaga (Flavored Meat and Potatoes)

Ingredients (for 4 persons)
  4 medium potatoes
      (1 pound/450g)
  7 ounces (200g) beef or
      pork, thinly sliced
  1 tablespoon finely
      chopped fresh ginger
  2 tablespoons sugar
  2 tablespoons *sake*
  3 tablespoons soy sauce

①Pare potatoes and cut into 4–6 pieces. Soak in water for 5 minutes.
②Cut thinly sliced meat into 1½–2-inch (4–5 cm) pieces.
③Mix sugar, soy sauce, *sake* and ginger and bring to a boil. Add meat and bring to a boil again. Add potatoes and water to cover, and place a lid inside right on the ingredients (picture 1/see page 71). Bring to a boil again, then simmer till potatoes are cooked.

Beef Flavored with Soy Sauce and Ginger

Ingredients (for 4 persons)
  ¾ pound (340g) beef,
      thinly sliced
  ¼ cup finely slivered
      fresh ginger
  ⅚ cup (200ml) *dashi* (see
      page 17)
  2 tablespoons sugar
  3⅓ tablespoons *sake*
  2½ tablespoons soy sauce

①Cut beef into 1½-inch (4 cm) squares.
②Place beef and ginger in saucepan. Add enough *dashi* broth to cover beef, then add sugar, *sake,* soy sauce and simmer. Stirring occasionally, cook until scarcely any broth is left.

Note: This dish can also serve as flavorful ingredient for *ocha-zuke* (see page 26).

1 Cooking with a lid placed inside.

Sauteed Pork with Ginger

This is a quick dish to prepare — just saute seasoned, thinly sliced pork. This dish, which is relatively inexpensive and yet rich in taste, is very popular in every home.

Ingredients (for 4 persons)
¾ pound (340g) pork (shoulder butt) thinly sliced

Dipping sauce
3 tablespoons soy sauce
2 tablespoons *sake*
2 teaspoons grated fresh ginger (pictures 1 & 2)

2 tablespoons vegetable oil

①Combine dipping sauce ingredients.

②Cut pork into 2-inch (5 cm) pieces and steep in sauce for 10 minutes. Do not oversteep or the pork will become tough.

③Heat vegetable oil in skillet and saute pork (spreading out the slices) over high heat till slightly brown; then turn and saute at medium heat. Add remaining sauce, and cook for 1–2 minutes.

Note: It is often served with sauteed green peppers or with fresh lettuce and tomato. The relish illustrated in the photograph is small green peppers sauteed with salt and pepper.

1 Scrape off ginger skin with a spoon or knife.

2 Use a fine grater and grate quickly.

Tonkatsu (Breaded Pork Cutlets)

This is a western style meat dish which is often prepared at home.

Ingredients (for 4 persons)
  4 pork loin cutlets
       (½-inch/1cm thick,
       about 4 ounces/120g
       each)
  1 teaspoon salt
  pepper
  2 tablespoons flour
  1 egg
  1 cup dried bread
       crumbs
  vegetable oil for deep
     frying
  Shredded cabbage
  Tonkatsu sauce
  Japanese mustard

① To prepare pork: make 2–3 short cuts across the line separating meat and fat (picture 1), and pound with a meat pounder to tenderize. Sprinkle with salt and pepper on both sides arranging at the same time the shape to the original.

② Dust with flour evenly and shake off excess flour. Dip into whisked egg and then coat with dried bread crumbs evenly (picture 2). Press with hands to settle bread crumbs on pork.

③ Shred cabbage and soak in water for 5 minutes to crisp. Drain.

④ Heat enough oil to cover meat (320°–340°F/160°–170°C). Slide in breaded pork (picture 3) and fry till the underside turns golden brown; then turn over. Frying time is about 5–6 minutes. Raise the oil temperature to 360°F (180°C) for the last minute of frying for a crispy finish. Do not fry too many pieces at one time.

⑤ Mound shredded cabbage in a serving dish. Cut fried pork into bite-size pieces. Ladle *tonkatsu* sauce (see note) over the pork. Serve with Japanese mustard.

Note: *Tonkatsu* sauce is thicker than Worcestershire sauce and richer in flavor. If commercial *tonkatsu* sauce is not available, make your own as follows: Mix 4 tablespoons tomato catsup, 2 tablespoons Worcestershire sauce, and 2 tablespoons white wine in a saucepan. Boil and let cool.

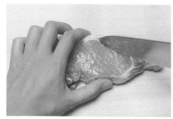

1 Make 2—3 short cuts at the line between meat and fat.

2 Coat with bread crumbs evenly.

3 Slide in breaded meat from edge of skillet.

Fried Chicken Seasoned with Soy Sauce and Ginger

Chicken is seasoned with soy sauce and ginger before frying. This is Japanese-style fried chicken.

Ingredients (for 4 persons)
1¼ pounds (570g) chicken thigh, boned
2 tablespoons soy sauce
2 tablespoons *sake*
2 teaspoons fresh ginger juice (see page 49)
5 tablespoons potato or corn starch
vegetable oil for deep-frying

① Using a fork, prick holes all over the chicken (picture 1). Cut into 2-inch (5 cm) pieces.

② Mix soy sauce, *sake* and fresh ginger juice. Steep chicken in the soy sauce mixture for 20 minutes, stirring occasionally (picture 2).

③ Pat chicken dry with a paper towel and coat thinly with starch.

④ Heat vegetable oil to 330°–340°F (165°–170°C) and fry slowly and well.

1 Prick holes all over the chicken.

2 Turn over chicken in soy sauce mixture.

Yakitori (Skewered, Grilled Chicken)

Yakitori is so popular that it is an almost indispensable dish in most Japanese drinking places. It is also ofen served at parties.

Ingredients (for 4 persons)

10 ounces (300g) chicken thigh, boned
10 ounces (300g) chicken wing, boned
½ pound (230g) chicken liver
2 long onions
16 small green peppers
½ teaspoon salt

Yakitori sauce
4 tablespoons sugar
½ cup (120ml) *mirin*
½ cup (120ml) soy sauce
lemon
sansho (powdered Japanese pepper)
shichimi-togarashi (powdered red pepper mixed with six other spices)
bamboo skewers

① Soak liver in plenty of water for 15–30 minutes to remove blood.

② Cut chicken (thigh and wings) and liver into bite-size pieces. Mount 4 pieces each onto bamboo skewers.

③ Cut long onions into 2-inch pieces and mount onto bamboo skewers. The same with small green peppers.

④ To make *yakitori* sauce: Mix sugar, *mirin,* and soy sauce and boil till reduced to ⅔ original amount (picture 1).

⑤ Grill skewered meat and vegetable pieces over open fire as in a barbecue (picture 2/see note). Brush meat with *yakitori* sauce 2–3 times while grilling (picture 3). For vegetables, brush once with sauce, and grill. Grill some of the skewered pieces simply sprinkled with salt.

⑥ Place in a serving dish and serve with lemon juice, *sansho* or *shichimi-togarashi.*

Note: Soaking bamboo skewers in salted water before using helps keep them from burning.

1   Boil *yakitori* sauce till reduced to ⅔.

2   Grill skewered meat and vegetable pieces over open fire.

3   Brush on *yakitori* sauce 2–3 times while grilling.

Noshidori (Fan-shaped Chicken Loaf)

Chicken loaf is cut and pierced with a *tessen*-skewer, to look like a folded Japanese fan. The dish is often prepared for the New Year. It is also a delightful dish for parties.

Ingredients (for 15 pieces)
14 ounces (400g) chicken, ground
(A) 1 tablespoon soy sauce
    1 tablespoon *sake*
    1 teaspoon sugar
    1 teaspoon *mirin*
(B) 1 tablespoon sugar
    1 tablespoon soy sauce
    1 teaspoon fresh ginger juice (picture 1)
    1 tablespoon potato or corn starch
 1 egg
vegetable oil
2 teaspoons poppy seeds
tessen-skewer

① Mix half the ground chicken and (A) ingredients, and cook in heated skillet, stirring constantly, until the meat becomes crumbly.

② Put in an earthenware mortar and grind well. Add the remaining chicken and (B) ingredients and grind further. Add whisked egg slowly to form a paste. (A food processor can be used in place of a mortar)

③ Spread aluminum foil in a shallow 7 × 7 inch (18 × 18 cm) loaf pan and grease lightly. Pat chicken paste smooth into pan. Bake in oven at about 360°F (180°C) for 15 minutes.

④ Roast poppy seeds in dry skillet for 1–2 minutes. Be careful, for they burn easily.

⑤ Remove aluminum foil and cut off edges of loaf. Cut into the shape illustrated in picture 2 of a folded Japanese fan. Sprinkle with poppy seeds and pierce with a *tessen*-skewer (picture 3).

1 Grate ginger and squeeze out juice.

2 Cut the loaf into rectangular pieces shaped like fans.

3 Pierce with a *tessen*-skewer.

Sashimi

This is one of the most typical of Japanese dishes in which raw fish and seafood are sliced and served with soy sauce, seasoned with grated *wasabi*. The most important point is to use very fresh, quality ingredients.

Ingredients (for 4 persons)
7 ounces (200g) very
     fresh tuna fillet
4 ounces (120g) very
     fresh squid body
¼ sheet roasted *nori*
     (dried laver)
Relish and condiments
6 ounces (170g) *daikon*
     (Japanese radish)
wasabi, grated or paste
     (see page 7)
soy sauce

① Cut tuna into ¾ × 2 × 6–8-inch (2 × 5 × 15–20 cm) blocks along lines of muscles (picture 1). Slice blocks crosswise ½-inch (1 cm) thick with very sharp knife (picture 2).

② Cut squid top to open and flatten. Cut into 3-inch (7 cm) wide pieces lengthwise. Make several slashes, half as deep as the thickness of the squid. Place each piece slashed side underneath, place toasted *nori* on top and roll tightly (picture 3). Place roll with the seam down and cut into ½-inch (1 cm) thick pieces (see note).

③ Cut *daikon* into very thin strips (see page 37), crisp in water. Drain.

④ Place *daikon* strips in a serving dish, arrange tuna slices and squid rolls and add grated or paste *wasabi* on the side. Put a little soy sauce in a small dish. Garnish *sashimi* pieces with a bit of *wasabi* and dip into sauce before eating.

Note: Besides making into rolls, squid can simply be cut into thin slices. Slant knife slightly when cutting.

Besides *daikon,* seaweed, *shiso* leaves and/or grated *wasabi* and ginger commonly accompany *sashimi* to offset the fish smell.

1 Tuna should be cut lengthwise making into a rectanglar block.

2 Slice tuna blocks.

3 With slashed side underneath, roll squid with *nori* inside.

Bonito *Tataki* (Lightly Grilled Bonito with Condiments)

Being a migratory fish, the bonito moves northward towards Japan, riding the Japan current, in late spring. Partaking of the first bonito of the season is a time-honored custom for Japanese.

Ingredients (for 4 persons)

- 1 block bonito
  (¾ pound/340g)
- 1 teaspoon salt
- ¼ cup finely chopped
  scallions
- ⅔ cup grated *daikon*
- 1½ teaspoons grated fresh
  ginger
- 2 teaspoons fresh
  ginger, cut in fine
  strips
- 2 *shiso* leaves (beefsteak
  plant), cut in fine
  strips
- 1 lemon

① Prepare fish fillet cut lengthwise from the sides (picture 1). Slice away rib-bones (picture 2). Remove red flesh which runs lengthwise through the center (picture 3). One block is for 4 persons.

② Prepare each condiment. Cut lemon in half. Press the juice out of one half; cut the other half into wedges.

③ Place bonito, skin side down. Pass iron skewers crosswise through the block. Angle skewers so they are together at one end but apart at the other (picture 4).

④ Fill a large bowl with ice water. Grill bonito; first the skin side over a strong direct fire about 2 minutes (picture 5). When the skin is charred, turn over and grill the other side 1 minute.

⑤ Dip into ice water to cool quickly and take out. Remove the skewers with a rotating motion and dry bonito well with a cloth.

⑥ Place bonito on saranwrap, skin side down. Spread half the grated *daikon,* half the chopped scallions and the ginger strips evenly on top of bonito and sprinkle with juice of one-half lemon. With side of knife, lightly pound in condiments to help flavor seep in (picture 6). Fold up in saranwrap and refrigerate 40–50 minutes.

⑦ Remove condiments from bonito and place fish on cutting board, skin side up. Slice bonito into ½-inch (1 cm) thick pieces and arrange on a serving dish. Sprinkle with the remaining condiments. Each bonito slice, together with some condiments, is dipped into a small dish containing soy sauce when eating.

Note: If desired, grated garlic can also be added to condiments.

1 Prepare fish fillet cut lengthwise from the sides.

2 Slice away rib-bones.

3 Cut off red flesh that lines center.

4 Pass skewers.

5 Grill the skin side first over a strong direct fire.

6 Pound lightly with side of knife.

Grilled Yellowtail with Teriyaki Sauce

Yellowtail is most often used for a *teriyaki* dish. Other ingredients are young-yellowtail, Spanish mackerel, squid and chicken.

Marinated *kabu* (small white turnip) are so arranged to look like chrysanthemum flowers. They keep well and make nice relishes for a New Year's dish or for other celebrations.

Ingredients (for 4 persons)
4 fillets yellowtail
(3 ounces/90g each)
Teriyaki sauce
1 tablespoon sugar
4 tablespoons soy sauce
2 tablespoons *mirin*

① To make *teriyaki* sauce:
Mix sugar, soy sauce, *mirin* in saucepan and bring to a boil; then reduce heat and simmer for 1 minute.

② Heat grid, then remove from heat and brush with oil. This will prevent fish from sticking to grid while being grilled.

③ First grill the side which is to be facing up when served over high heat for 10 seconds; then reduce heat to medium and continue to grill (picture 1). Turn over and grill. Brush with sauce and turn over to dry (picture 2). Brush with sauce on the other side and turn over to dry. Repeat 3-4 times.

④ Place fish in a serving dish as shown in the photograph, with the skin side facing away from the diner. Some kind of relish is usually served with the fish. Here *kikka-kabu* (marinated turnip) is added. The remaining sauce can be poured over the fish, if desired.

Note: When grilling the yellowtail, iron skewers can also be passed through the fillet to keep the shape.

Kikka-kabu (Marinated White Turnip)

Ingredients (for 4 persons)
8 small *kabu* (small white turnip)
salt
Marinade
½ cup (120ml) rice vinegar
2 tablespoons sugar

dried red pepper /
lemon peel or *yuzu* citron

① Pare *kabu*. Place *kabu* between 2 wooden chopsticks or pencil-size wooden sticks on a cutting board. Cut *kabu* crosswise till knife touches the chopsticks (leaving bottom part between the chopsticks uncut/picture 3). Make many cuts crosswise and changing the position of the chopsticks, make similar cuts lengthwise.

② Soak *kabu* in salt water containing 1 tablespoon salt per cup of water for 5–6 hours. Place a flat plate on top of the *kabu* to keep them from floating up.

③ Dry *kabu* well and marinate overnight.

④ Drain marinated *kabu* and arrange them to look like chrysanthemum flowers. Place small pieces of dried red pepper or lemon peel or *yuzu* citron peel on top.

1 Grill first the side that will face up when served.

2 Brush with sauce and grill to dry. Repeat 3-4 times.

3 Keep the knife from cutting completely through the *kabu*.

Soy Sauce and Vinegar Flavored Sardines

Marinated Fresh-Water Smelt

The added flavors of rice vinegar, *sake* (rice wine) and ginger remove the sardine smell. Marinated fresh-water smelt is good as an hors d'oeuvre. If refrigerated, it keeps for a week.

In both dishes the fish is prepared so that the bones become soft and can be eaten without removing, a rich source of calcium.

Soy Sauce And Vinegar Flavored Sardines

Ingredients (for 4 persons)
8 sardines (2 ounces/60g each)
¼ cup (60ml) rice vinegar
¼ cup (60ml) *sake*
¼ cup (60ml) soy sauce
3 tablespoons thinly cut fresh ginger

① Tear off the head of sardine by hand, remove entrails (picture 1) and clean thoroughly in water. Dry with a cloth and cut into 2–3 pieces crosswise.

② Bring *sake* and vinegar to a boil in an enameled-ware pot or a heat-proof glass pot. Arrange sardines in the pot, add fresh ginger and simmer 10 minutes with a lid placed right on the sardines (see page 71). Then, add soy sauce and continue simmering until scarcely any of the liquid is left.

Marinated Fresh-Water Smelt

Ingredients (for 4 persons)
20 fresh-water smelts (⅓ ounce/10g each)
potato or corn starch
vegetable oil for deep-frying
1 dried red pepper
2 long onions
Marinade
3 tablespoons rice vinegar
3 tablespoons *sake*
3 tablespoons soy sauce
3 tablespoons *mirin*
½ cup (120ml) water

① Clean fresh-water smelt under running water and dry with paper towel.

② To make marinade: Mix vinegar, *sake,* soy sauce, *mirin* and water. Bring to a boil; then pour into a flat glass container.

③ Soak dried red pepper in water to soften. Remove seeds (see page 6). Chop finely. Add to the marinade. Cut long onions into 1-inch (3 cm) lengths, broil on grid (or in skillet) over high heat till slightly burnt (picture 2); then add to the marinade.

④ Heat vegetable oil to 340°F (170°C). Coat smelt with starch, slide into oil, and fry until golden brown. Marinate the fish immediately after frying, while still hot, for 1–2 hours.

1 Remove entrails.

2 Broil long onion on heated grid till slightly burnt.

Grilled Clams Seasoned with Salt

Short-Necked Clams Steamed with Sake

In Japan, seafood is often eaten by simply grilling over an open fire and seasoning only with salt to enjoy the taste of the seafood itself.

Among shellfish recipes, short-necked clams steamed with *sake* is also very simple to prepare. Clams with shells tightly closed are considered fresh.

Grilled Clams Seasoned with Salt

Ingredients (for 4 persons)
12 clams
salt

① Immerse clams in salt water containing 1½ teaspoons salt per cup of water and place in a dark place for 5–6 hours (picture 1). Then clams will let out sand.

② Wash shells well by rubbing. Cut off the black spot at the hinge of shells to prevent shells from opening and letting juice spill out (picture 2). Sprinkle with salt.

③ Heat grid, place clams on top, cover with a bowl or aluminum foil sheet, and grill (picture 3). When salt dries and appears as a white crust on the shells, the clams are done.

Short-Necked Clams Steamed with Sake

Ingredients (for 4 persons)
1 pound (450g) short-necked clams with shell
½ cup (120ml) water
½ cup (120ml) *sake*
2 tablespoons finely chopped scallions or parsley

① Remove sand by soaking clams in salt water.

② Wash clams well in fresh water, rubbing shells against each other.

③ Place clams in a flat saucepan containing ½ cup (120 ml) water and *sake,* and steam. When clams open shells, remove from heat. Clams with unopened shells should be discarded.

④ Place clams with the broth in a deep serving dish and sprinkle with scallions or parsley. Serve warm.

1 Soak clams in water containing 3% salt.

2 Cut off the black spot at the hinge of shells.

3 Cover and grill.

Boiled Spinach with Sesame Dressing

Green Beans with Peanut Dressing

There are many kinds of vegetables with dressing. They make nice side dishes.

Roasting sesame seeds before grinding brings out the flavor.

Peanut butter is used here to simplify cooking, but ordinarily the dressing is made from ground roasted peanuts.

Boiled Spinach with Sesame Dressing

Ingredients (for 4 persons)
- ¾ pound (340g) spinach
- 5 tablespoons white sesame seeds
- 2 teaspoons *dashi* (see page 17)
- 1 tablespoon soy sauce

① Wash spinach thoroughly. Boil in a potful of water, with stalks at bottom and leafy parts at top, till soft. Drain and rinse well. Trim off spinach ends and squeeze out water (picture 1). Cut into 1½-inch (4 cm) lengths.

② Roast sesame seeds in a dry skillet over low heat, stirring constantly to prevent burning. When seeds begin to pop, remove (saving about 1 teaspoonful to use as garnish) to earthenware mortar and grind with pestle until the seeds are half-crushed (see page 6). Add soy sauce and *dashi,* mix well.

③ Loosen spinach. Add to the dressing, and mix well.

④ Place in a small bowl and garnish with roasted sesame seeds.

Note: Mix spinach and dressing just before serving. Mixing too far in advance makes the dish watery.
By substituting cabbage, wartercress or string beans for the spinach, similar dishes can be prepared.

Green Beans with Peanut Dressing

Ingredients (for 4 persons)
- ½ pound (230g) green beans
- ½ teaspoon soy sauce

Peanut dressing
- 3 tablespoons sugarless chunky peanut butter
- ½ tablespoon sugar
- ½ tablespoon soy sauce
- 1 tablespoon *dashi* (see page 17)

① String the beans. Cook uncovered in plenty of boiling water, until beans turn a bright green. Do not overcook. Drain, spread out and cool (picture 2). Cut diagonally into 1-inch (2 cm) lengths.

② To make dressing: mix well peanut butter, sugar, soy sauce and *dashi.*

③ Sprinkle ½ teaspoon soy sauce over the beans and let stand for 10 minutes. Mix into the peanut dressing.

1 Trim off the spinach ends and squeeze out water.

2 By cooling quickly, the bright color is retained.

Ohitashi

Grilled Eggplant

These are light and simple dishes, popular in every Japanese home.

Ohitashi can be substituted with *tsumamina* (rape-seedlings), *shungiku* (chrysanthemum leaves), *mitsuba* (trefoil) and *seri* (Japanese watercress).

Ohitashi

Ingredients (for 4 persons)
¾ pound (340g) spinach
3 tablespoons *dashi* (see page 17)
1 tablespoon soy sauce
dried bonito flakes

① Wash spinach thoroughly. Cook in plenty of boiling water, with stalks at bottom and leafy parts at top. Drain and rinse well. Trim off spinach ends and squeeze out water. Cut into 1½-inch (4 cm) lengths.

② Mix *dashi* and soy sauce.

③ Place spinach in a small bowl and pour *dashi* sauce over it. Garnish with bonito flakes.

Grilled Eggplant

Ingredients (for 4 persons)
6 Japanese-variety egg-plants (weighing about 2½ ounces/70g each)
1 tablespoon finely grated ginger
3⅓ tablespoons soy sauce
1 tablespoon *mirin*
1 tablespoon *sake*
¼ cup dried bonito flakes

① Grill eggplants on grid over high heat, turning to char all sides (picture 1).

② When eggplants become soft to the touch, put into cold water. Peel while still hot (picture 2). Cut off stem but leave top covering; cut into 5–6 strips from below covering. Do not leave in cold water too long.

③ Mix soy sauce, *mirin, sake,* and dried bonito flakes (reserve some flakes for garnish). Bring to a boil and strain.

④ Place eggplants in a deep serving dish. Sprinkle with bonito flakes and pour the soy sauce mixture over eggplants. Place some grated ginger on the side.

1 Grill eggplants on grid till soft.

2 Peel at once.

Namasu (Marinated Daikon and Carrots)

Cucumber and Squid
with Vinegar Dressing

The combination of red and white colors symbolizes celebration in Japan. *Namasu* made with red and white vegetables, is often prepared for festive events such as the New Year.

Cucumber and squid with vinegar dressing is a salad dish. A dish with a tart and simple taste is often added to complete a meal menu.

Namasu (Marinated Daikon and Carrots)

Ingredients (for 4 persons)
¾ pound (340g) *daikon*
    (Japanese radish)
1 ounce (30g) carrots
3 tablespoons rice
    vinegar
1 tablespoon *dashi* (see
    page 17)
1 tablespoon *mirin*
2 teaspoons sugar
salt

① Cut *daikon* crosswise into 2-inch (5cm) thick pieces. Pare and cut each piece lengthwise into thin slices; then cut slices again lengthwise into fine strips. Do the same with carrots. Sprinkle with a pinch of salt evenly over *daikon* and carrots and let stand in a basket for 10–15 minutes till limp.

② Squeeze *daikon* and carrots to remove water.

③ Mix vinegar, *dashi, mirin* and sugar and add a pinch of salt. Marinate *daikon* and carrots in the vinegar mixture. It can be served immediately, but marinating for a day will make it more zesty.

Cucumber and Squid with Vinegar Dressing

Ingredients (for 4 persons)
1 middle sized squid
    (7 ounces/200g),
    fresh or frozen
2 Japanese-variety
    cucumbers
    (7 ounces/200g)
1 teaspoon salt
Sanbai-zu (vinegar dressing)
1 tablespoon sugar
4 tablespoons rice
    vinegar
1 tablespoon *dashi* (see
    page 17)
2 teaspoons *mirin*
2 teaspoons soy sauce
1 tablespoon finely sliv-
    ered fresh ginger,
    soaked in water

① Pull out legs and entrails of squid. Peel off skin from the top part (body) and cut open to flatten out. Cut decorative slashes on the surface lengthwise and crosswise to half the thickness (picture 1). Cut slashes diagonally on squid legs so they will scroll when boiled.

② Boil squid legs and body together lightly. Cut body into rectangular pieces, ½-inch by 2-inch (1 × 5cm).

③ Sprinkle with ½ teaspoon salt over cucumber and roll over on cutting-board to remove pricks (picture 2). Wash lightly and slice thinly crosswise. Sprinkle with ½ teaspoon salt and let stand for 10 minutes. When cucumber becomes limp, squeeze out water.

④ Mix sugar, vinegar, *dashi, mirin* and soy sauce for *sanbai-zu* (vinegar dressing/see note). Pour 1 tablespoon vinegar dressing over cucumber and squid.

⑤ Just before serving, drain watery vinegar dressing and place cucumber/squid in a serving dish; pour over the remaining dressing. Decorate with strips of ginger on top.

Note:　*Sanbai-zu* means a dressing consisting of three flavors: tart, salty and sweet. Vinegar is used for sour flavor; salt, soy sauce is used for salty flavor; and sugar, *mirin,* for sweet flavor.

1　Cut slashes on the squid top (body).

2　Roll by hand on cutting-board.

Root Vegetables with Chicken

This dish is made by cooking various root vegetables and chicken together with a rich, thick flavored sauce.

Ingredients (for 4 persons)
- 6 *sato-imo* (taro)
  (¾ pound/340g)
- ½ carrot (¼ pound/120g)
- ½ burdock root
  (¼ pound/120g)
- ⅔ section lotus root
  (¼ pound/120g)
- 6 ounces (170g) chicken
- ⅔ block *konnyaku*
- 1½ tablespoons sesame
  oil
- 1 cup (240 ml) *dashi* (see
  page 17)
- 1½ tablespoons sugar
- 2 tablespoons *mirin*
- 2 tablespoons *sake*
- 3 tablespoons soy sauce
- 2 tablespoons green
  peas (frozen or
  canned)

① Pare *sato-imo* thickly. Rub with salt and rinse well in water to remove slime from surface (picture 1). Cut all ingredients into bite-size pieces (picture 2). Soak lotus root and burdock root in water immediately to keep from discoloring (picture 3). Boil *konnyaku* lightly.

② Heat sesame oil in a heavy pot and saute vegetables and *konnyaku*. Add chicken and saute further till chicken turns color. Then add *dashi*, sugar, *mirin* and *sake* and cook until the *dashi* is greatly reduced. Add soy sauce and continue to cook, stirring constantly.

③ Pour boiling water over green peas and drain.

④ Place all ingredients in a serving dish. Sprinkle green peas on top.

1 Sprinkle salt over *sato-imo* and rub.

2 Turning carrot, cut diagonally.

3 Soak lotus root and burdock root in water immediately.

Kimpira-Gobo (Sauteed Burdock Flavored with Soy Sauce)

Sauteed Celery Flavored with Soy Sauce

Kimpira-Gobo is a popular dish which reminds many Japanese of their mother's cooking. It keeps well. This dish is ideal as a relish for *sake* or as a side dish in a boxed lunch with rice.

Kimpira-Gobo (Sauteed Burdock Flavored with Soy Sauce)

Ingredients (for 4 persons)
- ¾ burdock root
  (5 ounces/140g)
- ½ carrot (2 ounces/60g)
- 1½ tablespoons sesame oil
- 1 tablespoon sugar
- ½ tablespoon *mirin*
- 1 tablespoon soy sauce
- 4 tablespoons *dashi* (see page 17)
- 1 dried red pepper
- 1 tablespoon white sesame seeds

① Wash burdock root and scrape off the thin, brown skin with back of knife (picture 1). Cut into 2-inch (5 cm) matchsticks (picture 2). Soak in water immediately to prevent change of color.

② Pare carrots and cut into strips of the same length and thickness as the burdock.

③ Roast sesame seeds in a dry skillet over low heat, stirring constantly to prevent burning. When seeds begin to pop, transfer to a dry bowl.

④ Soak dried red pepper in water to soften. Cut in half and squeeze out seeds under water (see page 6). Chop finely.

⑤ Drain burdock and pat dry with paper towel.

⑥ Heat sesame oil in saucepan. Saute burdock and carrots over high heat. Add sugar, *mirin,* soy sauce and *dashi* and reduce heat to medium.
Cook until all liquid is absorbed (picture 3). Add red pepper and sesame seeds and mix well.

⑦ Place in a bowl, arranging into a mound.

Note: You may use a peeler to pare the burdock instead of scraping with the back of a knife but this removes the full flavor of the vegetable which lies just under the skin.

Adding pork strips will make the dish more zesty. Similar dishes can be prepared by substituting lotus root, potato, green pepper, or celery for the burdock.

Sauteed Celery Flavored with Soy Sauce

Ingredients (for 4 persons)
- 4 celery stalks (including leafy part)
- 1 tablespoon oil
- 1½ tablespoons *sake*
- 1 teaspoon sugar
- 1½ tablespoons soy sauce
- 1½ teaspoons *mirin*

① Cut celery stalks and leaves into ¾-inch (2 cm) long pieces. Boil till slightly soft.

② Heat oil and saute celery.

③ Add *sake,* sugar, soy sauce, *mirin* and cook over medium heat, stirring until all liquid is gone.

1 Scrape off the thin, brown skin with back of knife.

2 Cut burdock into 2-inch (5 cm) matchsticks.

3 Cook until all liquid is absorbed.

Flavored Pumpkin

Sugar Flavored Kidney Beans

In Japan, we have a saying that if we eat pumpkin on the winter solstice (the shortest day of the year) we will not catch cold through the winter. It was known from olden days that pumpkin was a good source of carotin.

Dried beans cooked with sugar and/or soy sauce are served as a small side dish.

Flavored Pumpkin

Ingredients (for 4 persons)
1¼ pounds (570g) pumpkin
1¼ cups (300 ml) *dashi*
    (see page 17)
2 tablespoons *mirin*
¼ teaspoon salt
½ tablespoon soy sauce

① Halve or quarter pumpkin and remove seeds and stringy part. Cut into 2-inch (5 cm) pieces. Slice off skin at random to give surface a mottled look and to enable flavor of *dashi* to steep in (picture 1).

② Put pumpkin in saucepan with the skin side down, and add *dashi.* Bring to a boil; add *mirin* and cook over low heat for 5 minutes with ''dropped-lid'' placed right on the ingredients (see note and picture 2). Add salt and soy sauce.
Cover with saucepan lid. Simmer till soft and most of the liquid evaporates. Turn off heat and cool in saucepan to let the flavor steep in.

Note: The ''dropped-lid'' technique is often used in Japanese cooking. A smaller lid is placed right on the ingredients. This lid keeps the ingredients from crumbling and helps spread the flavor of the broth evenly, without stirring.
A wooden lid or aluminum lid is used for this purpose. For delicate ingredients, use a piece of aluminum foil or waxed paper with a hole cut in the center to let steam out.

Sugar Flavored Kidney Beans

Ingredients (for 4 persons)
5¼ ounces (150g) dried
    kidney beans
⅘ cup sugar
⅕ teaspoons salt

① Wash and pick over kidney beans. Cover beans with 6 cups water in a large pot and soak 5–6 hours.

② Put the pot of beans in the water over a low flame and bring to gentle boil; then turn up to medium heat and boil 5 minutes. Discard water. Add just enough hot water to cover beans and simmer 1 hour with a lid placed right on the beans. Add more hot water as needed to keep beans covered.

③ Divide the sugar into three. Cook beans over a low flame for another hour, adding one-third of the sugar at a time. When beans become soft, add salt and turn off heat. Leave as is for a while to let flavor steep in.

Note: Soybeans flavored with soy sauce and a little sugar is a similar popular dish.

When canned beans are used, put just enough water to cover and cook, following the instruction from #③.

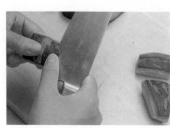

1 Slice off skin at random.

2 Place a ''dropped lid''.

Eggplant and Green Peppers Sauteed with Miso

Vegetable oil and *miso* go very well with eggplants. In Japan, summer is the season for eggplants and green peppers grown outdoors. They help stimulate lagging appetites on hot summer days.

Ingredients (for 4 persons)
- 5 Japanese-variety eggplants
  (¾ pound/340g)
- 3 green peppers
  (¼ pound/120g)
- 4 tablespoons sesame oil
- 2½ tablespoons *miso*
- 1 tablespoon sugar
- 2 tablespoons *mirin*
- 2 teaspoons *sake*
- 2 teaspoons *dashi* (see page 17)

① Cut off stem and top covering of eggplants and pare lengthwise, leaving alternate stripes of skin (picture 1). Cut into ½-inch (1 cm) thick slices crosswise. Soak in water for 5 minutes and drain.

② Remove seeds from green peppers and cut into bite-size pieces.

③ Heat sesame oil in skillet and saute eggplants over high heat; add green peppers and saute further.

④ When eggplants and green peppers become soft, add *miso* and sugar, and saute until *miso* becomes slightly burnt (picture 2). Add *mirin, sake, dashi* and cook on medium heat, stirring, until scarcely any liquid remains.

1. Pare lengthwise, leaving alternate stripes of skin.

2. Saute until *miso* becomes slightly burnt.

Quick-pickled Vegetables (3 varieties)

Cabbage Pickles

Kabu Pickles

Daikon Pickled with Soy Sauce

Pickles prepared in quick fashion make a handy side dish that goes very well with rice. Since pickles can keep for 2–3 days if refrigerated, it is advisable to prepare a large amount at one time.

Daikon Pickled with Soy Sauce

Ingredients
- ⅓ *daikon* (Japanese radish/¾ pound/340g)
- 1 dried red pepper
- ½ cup (120ml) soy sauce
- ¼ cup (60ml) *sake*
- 2 tablespoons *mirin*
- 4 -inch (10cm) long *konbu*

① Cut *daikon* into 2-inch (5 cm) long pieces, pare and cut each piece in half lengthwise. Cut diagonal slashes on the curved surface (picture 1).

② Remove seeds from red pepper (see page 6) and chop.

③ Mix soy sauce, *sake* and *mirin* in a bowl and add *konbu* and red pepper.
Place *daikon* with the slashed side down in the soy sauce mixture, weigh down with about two plates on top and let sit for 2–3 hours (picture 2).

④ Cut pickled *daikon* into ½-inch (1 cm) thick slices and place in a serving dish.

Note: The soy sauce mixture can be used 2–3 times with different ingredients.

Kabu Pickles

Ingredients
- 1¼ pounds (570g) *kabu* (small white turnip) with leaves
- 2 teaspoons salt
- 2 -inch (5cm) long *konbu*
- 2 teaspoons finely slivered fresh ginger
- 2½ tablespoons soy sauce
- 2 tablespoons *mirin*
- 1 tablespoon *sake*
- 3 tablespoons dried bonito flakes

① Cut *kabu* leaves into 1½–2-inch (4–5 cm) lengths. Put through boiling water, then cold water, and squeeze out water. Cut *kabu* into bite-size wedges.
Sprinkle with salt over *kabu* and leaves and let stand for 20 minutes.

② Moisten *konbu* and cut into thin strips.

③ Mix soy sauce, *mirin* and *sake* in a bowl and add *kabu*, *kabu* leaves, *konbu*, ginger and dried bonito flakes. Weigh down with several plates on top and let stand for 30 minutes to 1 hour. Turn ingredients over once in the process.

Cabbage Pickles

Ingredients
- ¾ pound (340g) cabbage
- 1 Japanese-variety cucumber
- 1 tablespoon fresh ginger, chopped
- 3 *shiso* leaves (beefsteak plant)
- 2 tablespoons salt

① Cut cabbage into ½-inch (1 cm) wide pieces. Cut cucumber into thin slices (If using a regular cucumber, peel, quarter lengthwise, and seed). Cut *shiso* leaves into ¼-inch (0.5 cm) pieces.

② Put cucumbers in a bowl, sprinkle with salt and let sit for 5 minutes. Add remaining vegetables and crumple up with the hands till vegetables become watery and soft.

③ Rinse in water to remove salty taste. Squeeze out water and chill in refrigerator for 30 minutes. Sprinkle with a little soy sauce before eating.

1 Make diagonal slashes.

2 Weigh down with plates on top.

Fresh Tofu with Condiments

Ingredients (for 4 persons)
- 2 blocks *tofu*
  (1½ pounds/700g)

Tosa Joyu (dipping sauce)
- ½ cup (120ml) soy sauce
- 2 tablespoons *sake*
- ⅔ cup dried bonito flakes

Condiments
- 1 tablespoon grated
  fresh ginger
- 1 tablespoon *wasabi*
  grated or paste (see
  page 6)
- ½ cup finely chopped
  long onion
- 5 *shiso* leaves (beefsteak
  plant)
- ½ sheet of *nori* (dried
  laver)

Preparation is very simple and yet, a well chilled dish is a delight on hot summer days. Condiments are used to enhance the taste of *tofu*. One or more kinds can be used to suit individual taste.

① Put all ingredients for *Tosa joyu* in saucepan and bring to a boil. Strain through cheesecloth and cool in the refrigerator.

② Prepare condiments.
Soak finely chopped long onion in water and drain. Cut *shiso* leaves into thin strips. Using a pair of scissors, cut *nori* into thin strips.

③ Cut *tofu* into bite-size pieces. Shortly before serving, place in ice water to chill.

④ Place *tofu* in individual serving dishes, put condiments on top and pour *Tosa joyu* over. One or more kinds of condiments can be used at one time, but do not use ginger and *wasabi* together.

Note: *Tosa joyu* (dipping sauce) is suggested here, but the dish is more commonly served simply with soy sauce and condiments.

Boiled Tofu with Condiments

Ingredients (for 4 persons)

2 blocks *tofu*
   (1½ pounds/700g)
8 -inch (20cm) long
   konbu

Flavored sauce

⅓ cup (80ml) *dashi*
⅓ cup (80ml) soy sauce

Condiments

½ cup dried bonito flakes
½ cup finely chopped
   long onion
1 tablespoon roasted
   and roughly chopped
   white sesame seeds
½ cup grated *daikon* with
   red pepper (see
   page 6)

As with chilled fresh *tofu* with condiments, you can best enjoy the taste of *tofu* itself in this simple dish. Since it is served hot immediately after it is cooked at the dinner table, this is a very popular dish in winter.

① Wipe off *konbu* lightly. Soak in saucepan half-filled with water for 30 minutes.

② Cut *tofu* into bite-size pieces. Be careful not to let the *tofu* crumble.

③ Prepare condiments.
Soak long onion in water and drain. Roast sesame seeds in dry skillet over low heat. When sesame seeds begin to pop, turn off heat. Chop seeds roughly.

④ Mix *dashi* and soy sauce to make flavored sauce.

⑤ Place the saucepan containing the water used for soaking *konbu* on electric hot-plate at the dinner table. Place a small container with flavored sauce in the saucepan. When the water begins to a boil, put in a few pieces of *tofu* at a time and continue to boil. When *tofu* begins to shake, scoop out into a small serving bowl, pour sauce over *tofu* and add condiments to individual taste before serving.

Note: Be careful not to cook *tofu* too long or it will lose its best texture.

Grilled Tofu Flavored with Miso

This dish is best from late winter through spring when the fragrance of pepper buds mixed with *miso* dressing may be enjoyed.

Ingredients (for 4 persons)
2 blocks *momen-tofu*
   (1½ pounds/700g)
½ cup (120g) *miso*
1 tablespoon sugar
2 tablespoons *mirin*
4 tablespoons *dashi*
   (see page 17)
2 ounces (60g) spinach
   (leafy part)
5 *kinome/sansho* leaves
   (Japanese pepper
   buds)
2 tablespoons white
   sesame seeds

Dengaku-skewer

Kinome/sansho leaves

① Wrap *tofu* in a cloth and place between slightly tilted flat pans for 20–30 minutes to drain water (picture 1).

② Mix *miso,* sugar and *mirin,* blend in *dashi* stock and cook till smooth and creamy, stirring constantly.

③ Boil spinach, cut into small pieces and squeeze out water. Put spinach and buds into earthenware mortar and grind well. Add half the *miso* mixture and grind further. Put the ground mixture into a bowl.

④ Roast sesame seeds in dry skillet and grind in mortar (see page 6). Add the remaining *miso* mixture and mix, grinding.

⑤ Cut each *tofu* block into 6 pieces, broil in a greased pan 460°F (240°C) for 4–5 minutes. Spread *miso* dressing (one kind on some, the other on the rest/picture 2) and broil again until slightly burnt. Pass a skewer through each *tofu* piece and arrange on a serving dish.

Note: Ingredients with strong fragrance should be mixed in with *miso* dressing. In place of pepper buds used here, basil, parsley or lemon peel may be ground together with *miso* mixture.

1 Remove excess water from *tofu*.

2 Spread *miso* dressing on *tofu* block.

Fried Tofu with Grated Daikon and Ginger

Since this dish is best served while steaming hot, *tofu* should be coated with flour and be ready for frying immediately before serving.

Ingredients (for 4 persons)
2 blocks *tofu*
    (1½ pounds/700g)
flour
vegetable oil for deep-
    frying
Dashi sauce dressing
1 cup (240ml) *dashi* (see
    page 17)
½ tablespoon *mirin*
2 tablespoons soy sauce
Condiments
1 cup (240ml) grated *dai-
    kon* (see page 6)
1 tablespoon grated
    fresh ginger (see
    page 7)

① To remove excess water: wrap *tofu* in a clean, dry cloth, place on slightly tilted flat pan and place a light weight on top of the *tofu* for 10 minutes (see page 79).

② Mix ingredients for *dashi* sauce dressing and bring to a boil.

③ Heat frying oil to 360°F (180°C). Cut *tofu* into 4–6 blocks, coat with flour, and fry until they turn golden (picture 1). Drain on a rack.

④ Place *tofu* on a serving dish and cover with hot *dashi* sauce dressing. Place grated *daikon* and ginger on top.

Note: It is very important to remove as much excess water from the *tofu* as possible so it will not spatter while being cooked in oil. Corn starch may be used in place of flour.

1 Fry *tofu* blocks until they turn golden.

Scrambled Tofu

Sauteed Okara with Chicken and Vegetables

In the process of making *tofu* you get soybean milk and *okara* (tofu lees) as side-products. *Okara* is a health food, containing nutritive substances of soybeans as well as a high fiber content.

Scrambled Tofu

Ingredients (for 4 persons)
- 1 block *tofu*
  (¾ pound/340g)
- 2 dried Chinese black mushrooms
- ¼ burdock root
  (1½ ounces/50g)
- ½ carrot (1½ ounces/50g)
- ¼ pound (120g) chicken
- ½ long onion
  (1½ ounces/50g)
- 2 tablespoons vegetable oil
- ½ tablespoon *mirin*
- 2 tablespoons soy sauce
- 1 teaspoon sugar

Sauteed Okara with Chicken and Vegetables

Ingredients (for 4 persons)
- 7 ounces (200g) *okara* (*tofu* lees)
- 3 dried Chinese black mushrooms
- 1 sheet thin deep-fried *tofu*
- ¼ pound (120g) mixed vegetables (carrots, burdock root, boiled bamboo sprouts)
- ½ long onion
- ¼ pound (120g) chicken
- 2 tablespoons sesame oil
- 1¼ cups (300ml) *dashi*(see page 17/including water used for soaking dried Chinese black mushrooms)
- 1 tablespoon sugar
- 2 tablespoons *sake*
- 2 tablespoons *mirin*
- 2 tablespoons soy sauce
- ½ teaspoon salt
- 1 egg

① Break up *tofu* block into large pieces, boil lightly and drain on a dishcloth spread over colander (picture 1).

② Soak dried mushrooms in water to soften and cut into 1-inch (3 cm) long thin strips. Cut carrot likewise. Shave burdock into thin strips (see page 23). Cut chicken into ½-inch (1 cm) pieces. Chop long onion crosswise.

③ Heat oil in a saucepan, saute chicken, burdock, carrots and mushrooms until burdock becomes soft; then add *tofu* and mix thoroughly. Add *mirin,* soy sauce and sugar and cook further over high heat stirring constantly till all liquid is absorbed. Add long onion and turn off heat.

① Soak dried Chinese black mushrooms (see page 6) and cut into thin strips. Pour boiling water over fried *tofu* to remove excess oil and cut into 1½-inch (4 cm) long thin pieces. Cut carrots, burdock root and boiled bamboo sprout into thin strips. Chop long onion crosswise. Cut chicken into ½-inch (1 cm) pieces.

② Saute all ingredients but the long onion in sesame oil until soft; add *dashi*, sugar, *sake, mirin,* soy sauce and salt. Add *okara* and cook over medium heat for 3–4 minutes until scarcely any of the *dashi* mixture is left (picture 2). Add long onion and turn off heat.

③ Whisk egg and mix into ingredients; turn on heat again and cook lightly, stirring.

1 Drain boiled *tofu*.

2 Add *okara* and cook.

Egg Custard with Chicken, Shrimp and Vegetables

This is a custard-like dish in which eggs are blended with *dashi* and steamed. The knack to cooking this dish is to steam the egg mixture until it sets without making it porous.

Ingredients (for 4 persons)

3 eggs
2 cups (480ml) *dashi* (see page 17)
⅔ teaspoon salt
½ teaspoon soy sauce
1 teaspoon *mirin*

3 ounces (90g) chicken
soy sauce
sake

4 dried Chinese black mushrooms
¼ cup (60ml) water used for soaking mushrooms
¼ teaspoon sugar
½ teaspoon soy sauce
8 canned boiled ginkgo nuts
1 -inch (2.5cm) slice of *kamaboko* (boiled fish paste)
8 *mitsuba* (trefoil)

① Make *dashi* (see page 17). Add salt, soy sauce and *mirin* to *dashi*, mix and cool.

② To prepare ingredients: (picture 1)
Chicken: cut into bite-size pieces and sprinkle soy sauce and *sake* over them.
Dried Chinese black mushrooms: soak in water (see page 6). Cut off stems. Cut large tops in half. Add sugar and soy sauce to ¼-cup (60 ml) water used for soaking mushrooms, and cook mushrooms till flavor steeps in well.
Ginkgo nuts: open can and drain.
Kamaboko: cut into 4 slices.
Mitsuba: cut into 1½-inch (4 cm) lengths.

③ Whisk eggs in a mixing bowl, blend in seasoned *dashi* and strain. Place all ingredients but *mitsuba* in individual cups and slowly pour in egg mixture.

④ Cover each cup with saranwrap in order to keep water drops from falling into cup while steaming.

⑤ Arrange cups in large pot; fill with hot water to ⅓ the height of the cups; and cover pot with lid (picture 2). Boil and steam over medium-low heat for 15–20 minutes. Be careful not to let water boil too vigorously. At the last, put in *mitsuba* which had been briefly dipped in boiling water. Insert a skewer; if clear broth comes out, the dish is done.

1 Prepare ingredients.

2 Place cups in a pot. Be careful: steam can scald!

Egg Roll

In this dish, whisked eggs are blended with *dashi* broth and cooked into a moist, spongy roll. This egg roll can be eaten as is or used as a sushi ingredient.

Ingredients (for 4 persons)
  6 eggs
  dashi (¼ of egg amount/
    see page 17)
  1 teaspoon sugar
  1 teaspoon *mirin*
  soy sauce
  salt
  vegetable oil
Condiments
  grated *daikon*
    (see page 6)
  soy sauce

① Whisk eggs. Mix sugar, *mirin,* a dash of soy sauce and salt in *dashi* broth, then blend in whisked eggs.

② Put 1 tablespoon oil in egg-cooking pan and heat over medium to low heat. Remove excess oil. Oil must be spread evenly to the four corners of the pan.

③ Drop a bit of egg mixture in pan. If it sizzles, the pan is ready for cooking. If the drop smokes, the pan is overheated; remove from heat and cool by placing on a wet dish towel.

④ Spoon in ⅓ egg mixture and spread out evenly. As it cooks it begins to bubble. Press down big bubbles with chopsticks (picture 1).

⑤ When half-done, fold into 3 from farther end and grease empty space in the pan (pictures 2 & 3). Slide folded egg to farther side (picture 4). Grease empty space made at nearer side.

⑥ Spoon ½ the remaining egg mixture in empty space. Lift up the folded egg slightly and spread out egg mixture underneath (picture 5). When half-done, fold with folded egg inside, making into a roll. Grease pan and add the remaining egg mixture; following the above steps, make the roll bigger.

⑦ When egg roll is done, place on *makisu* (thin bamboo mat) while hot and shape egg roll into a square or round roll (picture 6). Leave for 4–5 minutes to cool.

⑧ Cut egg roll into appropriate sized pieces and place in a serving dish. Add grated *daikon* on the side and sprinkle with a little soy sauce. The egg roll is eaten with a little grated *daikon* on it.

Note: If an egg-cooking pan is not available, a shallow skillet can be substituted.

1 Press down big bubbles and cook keeping surface smooth.

2 Fold into 3, folding from the farther end.

3 Grease empty space.

4 Slide egg to farther side and grease empty space.

5 Lift up folded egg slightly and spread egg mixture underneath.

6 Place on *makisu* and shape egg roll.

Noodles Cooked with Chicken and Vegetables

Buckwheat Noodles Served with Sauce Dip

Both *udon* (wheat noodles) and *soba* (buckwheat noodles) are well liked by the Japanese. A variety of ingredients are used here, but any which cannot be obtained may be omitted.

Noodles Cooked with Chicken and Vegetables

Ingredients (for 4 persons)
 ¾ pound (340g) dried
      udon (Japanese
      wheat noodles)
 4 small dried Chinese
      black mushrooms
 4 tablespoons water
      used for soaking
      mushrooms
 ½ tablespoon soy sauce
 1 tablespoon *mirin*
 4 ounces (120g) chicken
      breast meat
 2 teaspoons *sake*
 salt
 1 -inch (3cm) carrot
 4 ounces (120g) spinach
 2 eggs
 1 tablespoon *mirin*
 vegetable oil
 2-inch (5cm) *kamaboko*
 (boiled fish paste)
Soup
 5 cups (1.2l) *dashi* (see
      page 17)
 6 tablespoons soy sauce
 4 tablespoons *mirin*
Condiments
 yuzu citron peel
 shichimi-togarashi
 (powdered red pepper
 mixed with six other
 spices)

Buckwheat Noodles Served with Sauce Dip

Ingredients (for 4 persons)
 ¾ pound (340g) dried
      soba (Japanese
      buckwheat noodles)
Sauce dip
 ½ cup (120ml) *mirin*
 ½ cup (120ml) soy sauce
 2¼ cups (540ml) water
 1 cup dried bonito flakes
Condiments
 ¼ cup finely chopped
      long onion
 ½ sheet *nori* (dried laver)
 4 teaspoons *wasabi*,
      grated or paste (see
      page 6)
shichimi-togarashi

① To make soup:
Make *dashi* with *konbu* and dried bonito flakes (see page 17) and season with soy sauce and *mirin.*

② To prepare ingredients:
Dried Chinese black mushrooms: soak in water to soften (see page 6). Simmer in water used for soaking with soy sauce and *mirin* until liquid is absorbed.
Chicken: mix *sake* and a pinch of salt, cook chicken in covered pan. Cut into bite-size pieces.
Carrots: cut into 8 thin slices and make into a flower shape with a vegetable cutter. Boil in lightly salted water.
Spinach: boil in boiling water, rinse in cold water; then wring out water. Cut into 1½-inch (4 cm) long pieces.
Egg: whisk eggs, add *mirin* and a pinch of salt, and mix. Fry in lightly greased skillet and cut into 4 pieces.
Kamaboko : slice into 4.

③ Cook *udon* noodles in plenty of boiling water till soft. Control the temperature so as not to let water bubble over. Drain.

④ Place noodles in individual pre-warmed serving bowls. Arrange all ingredients on top, and pour piping hot soup over everything. Float small pieces of *yuzu* citron peel on top. Sprinkle *shichimi-togarashi,* if desired.

① To make sauce dip:
Put *mirin* in saucepan and bring to a boil. Add soy sauce, water, dried bonito flakes and bring to a boil again, then reduce heat and simmer for 2–3 minutes. Strain and cool.

② To make condiments:
Soak finely chopped long onion in water and drain. Cut *nori* into thin strips.

③ Boil *soba* in plenty of boiling water 3–8 minutes (according to directions on bag), stirring to keep from sticking. Test by pinching noodle between fingers (picture 1). Rinse well in water and drain.

④ In one hand hold a small serving cup containing sauce with condiments, pick up noodles with chopsticks and dip in the sauce (picture 2).

Note: The noodles cooked with chicken and vegetables can be replaced with *soba*.

1 When no hard core remains, noodles are done.

2 Pick up noodles with chopsticks and dip in the sauce.

Zoni (Soup with Rice Cakes)

Clear Soup Type

Miso Soup Type

Zoni is a traditional dish in Japan and even today it is prepared in almost every Japanese home for New Year's Day.

In addition to rice cakes, many different ingredients are used in this dish and they vary from region to region in Japan and even among individual homes. We introduce 2 common dishes.

Zoni—Clear soup type

Ingredients (for 4 persons)
- 3 ounces (90g) chicken breast
- *sake*
- 7 ounces (200g) *daikon* (Japanese radish)
- 2 ounce (60g) carrot
- 4 *sato-imo* (taro) (1 ounce/30g each)
- salt
- 4 fresh Chinese black mushrooms, wiped, stems removed
- 3 ounces (90g) *komatsuna* (or spinach)
- 4 rice cakes
- 4 cups (1 l) *dashi*
- 1 teaspoon salt
- 2 teaspoons soy sauce
- 2 teaspoons *sake*
- *yuzu* citron peel

① To prepare ingredients:
Chicken: slanting the knife, cut into bite-size slices. Sprinkle with a little *sake* and salt and boil for a minute.
Daikon : cut into ½ × 2-inch (1 × 5 cm) thin rectangular slices.
Carrots: cut into 8 thin slices. Cut each slice with a flower shape cutter, if available (picture 1).
Sato-imo : pare skin thickly. Sprinkle with salt and rub well to remove slime from surface. Rinse in water and boil till soft.
Komatsuna : boil lightly, rinse in cold water and squeeze out water. Cut into 1½-inch (4 cm) lengths.

② Place rice cakes on grid and toast on both sides until they turn light brown and swell out (picture 2).

③ Bring *dashi* to a boil; add salt, soy sauce, *sake* and all ingredients except rice cakes. Cook for 2–3 minutes.

④ Cut *yuzu* citron peel (picture 3).

⑤ Pass toasted rice cakes through boiling water and place one cake in each individual serving bowl. Scoop out all ingredients from soup and place on top of rice cake. Ladle soup over all ingredients in each bowl and place *yuzu* citron peel on top.

Zoni—Miso soup type

Ingredients (for 4 persons)
- 2 ounces (60g) *daikon*
- 4 *sato-imo*(taro) (1 ounce/30g each)
- 2 ounces (60g) burdock root
- 4 fresh Chinese black mushrooms, wiped, stems removed
- ⅓ block grilled *tofu* (4 ounces/120g)
- 4 ounces (120g) *kyona* (or spinach)
- 4 round or square rice cakes
- 4 cups (1 l) *dashi*
- 5 ounces (140g) *saikyo-miso* (sweet white miso)
- ½ teaspoon salt
- ½ cup dried bonito flakes
- *ao-nori* (powdered green laver)

① To prepare ingredients:
Daikon : cut in half lengthwise, then cut each piece into ½-inch (1 cm) thick slices crosswise, making into thin half-circle pieces. Boil lightly.
Sato-imo : pare, sprinkle with salt and rub. Rinse in water to remove slime from surface. Boil till soft.
Burdock root : pare and cut into 1½-inch (4 cm) lengths. Cut each piece into thin slices lengthwise, then boil.
Grilled *tofu* : cut into 4.
Kyona : boil lightly, rinse in cold water, and squeeze out water. Cut into 1½-inch (4 cm) lengths.

② Put rice cakes into boiling water and boil until soft, but keep their shape.

③ Boil *dashi*,blend in *miso* paste, add salt and all ingredients but *kyona* and cook for 2–3 minutes.

④ Place each rice cake in an individual serving bowl. Scoop out all ingredients from *miso* soup and place on top of rice cake and add *kyona*. Ladle *miso* soup over all ingredients in each bowl and sprinkle with dried bonito flakes and *ao-nori*.

1 Cut each thin carrot slice into a flower shape.

2 Toast rice cakes. When they begin to puff they are done.

3 Cut *yuzu* citron peel into decorative shapes like a pine needle.

Okonomi-yaki

This is a thin, flat cake of unsweetened batter flavored with *dashi* (bonito fish stock) and fried with bits of meat, seafood and vegetables. It may be thought of as a Japanese version of a pancake or crepe.

Ingredients (for 4 persons)
2 cups (240g) flour
1 teaspoon baking
   powder
salt
1 cup (240ml) *dashi* (see
   page 17)
2 large cabbage leaves
1 egg
4 ounces (120g) pork,
   ground
vegetable oil
Sauce and condiments to
individual taste
  Worcestershire sauce
  soy sauce
  mayonnaise
  tomato catsup
  mustard
  dried bonito flakes
  red pickled ginger,
    minced
  ao-nori (powdered green
    laver)

① Sift flour, baking powder and salt together into a large mixing bowl. Adding *dashi* a little at a time, mix flour swiftly until smooth. Do not over-mix. Cover the bowl with saranwrap and leave for 30 minutes (if left too long, batter will become sticky).

② Remove hard section of cabbage leaves and cut into thin strips. Add egg, ground meat and cabbage to batter and mix lightly (picture 1).

③ Grease heated skillet well. Pour in batter and flatten out with spatula (picture 2). When bubbles begin to form and the edges begin to dry, turn over and fry the other side. Brush over cake with sauce or mustard (picture 3). When cake begins to give off aroma, sprinkle with dried bonito flakes, red pickled ginger and/or *ao-nori* and turn off heat.

Note: Using equal volumes of cabbage and batter is basic to this dish. Cabbage and egg are always used. Red pickled ginger and *age-dama* (batter dregs left from making *tempura*) are also often used.

1 After leaving batter for 30 minutes, fold in ingredients.

2 Flatten out batter and ingredients with spatula or ladle.

3 Brush with sauce to individual taste.

Kakiage

Tempura

This is a typical Japanese deep-fried dish. Ingredients are coated thinly with batter and fried crisply in plenty of oil. They are served with *ten-tsuyu* sauce seasoned with condiments.

Ingredients

shrimp/sillago/small horse
   mackerel/squid body
eggplant/fresh Chinese
   black mushroom/carrot/
   lotus root/sweet potato/
   pumpkin/onion
   small green pepper
Batter (for 4 persons)
  1 egg and cold water
     added to make 1 cup
     (240ml)
  1 cup (120g) flour
vegetable oil for deep
  frying

Ten-tsuyu (sauce dip)
  ¼ cup (60ml) *mirin*
  ¼ cup (60ml) soy sauce
  ⅓ cup dried bonito flakes
  1 cup (240ml) water
Condiments
  grated *daikon* (see
    page 6)
  grated fresh ginger (see
    page 7)

① Preparation of ingredients: (picture 1)

Shrimp: peel, but leave tail and the first section of shell attached to tail. Remove black vein and make 3–4 short cuts across the belly. Cut off tip of tail and squeeze out water with knife (see pages 13, 21).

Sillago and small horse mackerel: cut off head, remove entrails and clean. Cut the back lengthwise to open and flatten out. Remove central bone and wipe dry.

Squid: insert fingers in top part (body), pull apart the section connecting entrails to body, and pull out entrails without breaking. Remove the triangular shaped top and peel off skin. Cut body lengthwise to open and flatten out. Remove back bone. Cut into bite-size pieces and make short cuts around the edge of each piece to prevent curling while being fried. Wipe dry and dust with flour. Legs and triangular shaped part will be used for another deep-fried dish, *kakiage*.

Vegetables: prepare as shown in picture 2 below: cut slashes on eggplants. Make cuts lengthwise on green peppers to keep from bursting in hot oil. Slice onion and pierce each slice with a toothpick to hold layers together. Soak eggplant, lotus root, sweet potato in water to remove harshness. Wipe dry.

② To make *ten-tsuyu* (sauce dip):

Heat *mirin* ; and add water, soy sauce, dried bonito flakes, and bring to a boil. Strain.

③ To make batter:(picture 3)

Mix whisked egg and cold water in a mixing bowl. Add an equal volume of sifted flour and mix lightly.

④ Heat oil to 330°—340°F (test by dropping a bit of batter into the oil. If it sinks half way, then comes back up to the surface, the oil temperature is right for frying). Vegetables should be fried first. Dip into batter and slide ingredients into oil (picture 4). Turn over a few times and when the coating turns golden, scoop out onto rack and drain. Heat oil to 360°F and fry seafood (see note).

⑤ Place fried ingredients on paper towels spread out on a serving dish to absorb excess oil. Dip in a small, individual serving bowl containing *ten-tsuyu* before eating.

Note: The batter ingredients must be well-chilled before mixing, and then mixed very lightly. Over-mixing makes the batter heavy. Fry only enough amount at one time to cover about half the surface of oil in order to allow the ingredients to move freely. It is important to keep the oil temperature constant while frying. Scoop out dregs of batter as they accummulate.

1 Prepare fish and seafood as shown here.

2 Cut vegetables as shown here.

3 Equal parts of flour and the cold water/egg mixture are mixed together.

4 Dip into batter and put in oil at once.

Kakiage

Ingredients (for 4 persons)
- ¼ pound (120g) scallops
- 1 tablespoon flour
- 1 ounce (30g) *mitsuba* (trefoil)
- ¼ pound (120g) shrimps, peeled
- 1 tablespoon flour
- 1 long onion
- 1 squid (legs and triangular-shaped part only)
- 1 tablespoon flour
- ½ onion
- 1 ounce (30g) snow peas

Batter
- 1 egg and cold water added to make ¾ cup (180ml)
- ¾ cup (90g) flour

vegetable oil for deep frying
ten-tsuyu (see *Tempura*)
condiments (see *Tempura*)

① Preparation of ingredients:
Scallops: cut into ½-inch (1 cm) pieces. Dry and dust with flour.
Shrimp: peel; wipe dry and dust with flour.
Squid legs and triangular-shaped part: cut off legs from entrails. Remove skin of legs (picture 1). Cut into ½-inch (1 cm) pieces. Cut the triangle into ½-inch (1 cm) pieces. Wipe dry and dust with flour.
Mitsuba: cut into 1-inch (2.5 cm) lengths.
Long onion: cut into ½-inch (1 cm) lengths.
Onion: cut into ½-inch (1 cm) cubes.
Snow peas: string and cut diagonally into thin strips.

② Prepare batter in a mixing bowl and divide into 3 portions: add scallops and *mitsuba* to one portion of batter and mix. Mix shrimp and long onion in another portion. Mix squid, onion and snow peas in the third (picture 2).

③ Heat oil to 320°F (160°C). With a ladle lightly scoop up about two tablespoons of the mixture, spread out on a wooden spatula, and slide the mixture into the oil (picture 3). As the mixture takes a firm shape in the hot oil, flatten out the ingredients to keep the thickness uniform. Turn 2–3 times.

Note: In *kakiage* many different combinations of seafood and vegetables can be enjoyed. Among popular combinations are small shrimps and green peas; *sakura-ebi* (dried small shrimp) and onion; squid and mixed vegetables. Almost any leftover ingredient can be made into *kakiage*, so it is a handy dish for cleaning out the refrigerator.

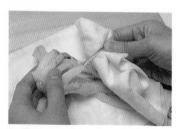

1 Remove skin of squid legs.

2 Mix batter with each portion of ingredients.

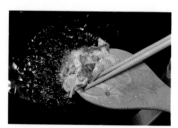

3 Slide the mixture into the oil.